HOMEMADE QUICK BREADS

Betty Crocker's

HOMEMADE QUICK BREADS

PRENTICE HALL

NEW YORK   LONDON   TORONTO   SYDNEY   TOKYO   SINGAPORE

PRENTICE HALL GENERAL REFERENCE
15 Columbus Circle
New York, New York 10023

Library of Congress Cataloging-in-Publication data
Crocker, Betty.
   [Homemade quick breads]
   Betty Crocker's homemade quick breads.
      p.   cm.
   Includes index.
   ISBN 0-671-84717-1
      1. Bread. 2. Muffins. 3. Biscuits. 4. Coffee
cakes. I. Title.   II. Title: Homemade quick breads.
   TX769.C744   1993
   641.8'15—dc20   92-25394
                                                    CIP

GENERAL MILLS, INC.
Betty Crocker Food and Publication Center
      Director, Marcia Copeland
      Editor, Diane Undis
      Recipe Development, Mary H. Johnson
      Food Stylist, Kate Courtney Condon
Nutrition Department
      Nutritionist, Nancy Holmes, R.D.
Photographic Services
      Photographer, Nanci Doonan Dixon

Designed by Nina D'Amario/Levavi & Levavi
Manufactured in the United States of America

First Edition

10 9 8 7 6 5 4 3 2 1

Cover: Blueberry Coffee Cake (page 58), Apple-Rhubarb Bread (page 73), Peanut Butter–Honey Muffins (page 16)
Preceding page: Raspberry-Peach Coffee Cake (page 67), Braided Cream Cheese Coffee Cake (page 64)

Contents

Introduction

Everyone loves fresh, warm muffins, biscuits and coffee cakes, but do we really have the time to make them from scratch? Absolutely! Quick breads are perfect for the way we bake today. People are rediscovering the joys of home-baked breads at a time when we are all busier than ever. You'll find that with Betty Crocker your favorite recipes are easy and surprisingly quick to prepare.

We love the convenience of quick breads. Most of these recipes need no time to rise—you just measure, mix and bake. Many muffins will be ready in about half an hour, including preparation *and* baking time. And nothing's better than a delicious, homemade muffin in the morning. Unless, of course, it's a tantalizing, deliciously sticky coffee cake, a perfect, buttery biscuit or a hearty slice of nut bread.

For this cookbook, we've gathered all of the very best recipes—from classics such as Blueberry Streusel Muffins and Buttermilk Biscuits, to new favorites such as Papaya-Custard Coffee Cake and Ginger-Pear Bread. There's a recipe here for every taste, every mood and every meal. From delicious berry treats in the summer, to festive cranberry and apple goodies in the winter, you'll be making delicious quick breads all year 'round.

There's also an entire chapter devoted to healthful recipes that include good-for-you grains. Each delicious recipe in this chapter is accompanied by thorough nutritional information. Try the Chocolate Chip–Date Coffee Cake, Ricotta-Spinach Muffins or Sour Cream Biscuits, and you just might change your idea of what "healthful" tastes like.

You'll love the extra features in this book whether you're a beginning baker or a pro. Gorgeous color photos throughout the book provide terrific ideas for presentation. And look for the special features in each chapter. You'll find tips for making perfect muffins, biscuits and breads, a chart of extra-easy, extra-quick muffins, tips on performing healthful "makeovers" on your favorite recipes, a photograph to help you identify grains that are growing in popularity and more.

There's just something irresistible about muffins, biscuits and coffee cakes, so we've really enjoyed working on this book. Try the many recipes in this collection; we're sure your family and friends will love them as much as we do!

The Betty Crocker Editors

1

Mouth-Watering Muffins

Muffins are almost a perfect food. They're easy and quick to make, portable and nicely self-contained. They can be a terrific excuse to eat lots of butter, honey or jam and they're just plain delicious! We usually think of breakfast as prime muffin time—there's a certain joy in waking up to warm blueberry or corn muffins. Even if you're the one waking up to make the muffins, you'll be amazed at how quickly they'll be ready to enjoy. By the time you're *really* awake, the muffins will be on the table.

But breakfast isn't the only time for muffins. Snacking on muffins is a time-honored tradition, and you can update the tradition by trying delicious new recipes. Raspberry-filled Chocolate Chip Muffins or Mocha Muffins, for example, might be your ultimate afternoon pick-me-up. You'll find that muffins can also be a so-phisticated alternative to bread with meals. Bake up a batch of muffins, put them on the table in a pretty basket, and suddenly the occasion is fun and festive. Double Corn Muffins are a terrific accompaniment for a barbecue dinner, Blue Cheese and Mushroom Muffins go well with omelettes and Parmesan-Tomato Muffins are perfect with a big main-dish salad.

Have fun trying different muffin sizes. On page 13, there's a chart to show you how to adapt your favorite recipes to make mini, generous bakery-style and jumbo muffins. You'll find that many of the recipes provide specific instructions on making different sizes, too. Mini muffins delight children, while jumbo muffins are for days when you have a jumbo appetite! We're sure you'll enjoy all of these muffins . . . no matter what the size or the occasion.

Blueberry Streusel Muffins (page 2)

Blueberry Streusel Muffins

Streusel Topping (below)
1 cup milk
¹/₃ cup vegetable oil
¹/₂ teaspoon vanilla
1 egg
2 cups all-purpose or whole wheat flour
¹/₃ cup sugar
3 teaspoons baking powder
¹/₂ teaspoon salt
1 cup fresh or frozen (thawed and well drained) blueberries

Heat oven to 400°. Grease bottoms only of 12 medium muffin cups, 2¹/₂ × 1¹/₄ inches, or line with paper baking cups. Prepare Streusel Topping; reserve.

Beat milk, oil, vanilla and egg in large bowl. Stir in flour, sugar, baking powder and salt just until flour is moistened. Fold in blueberries. Divide batter evenly among muffin cups (cups will be about ³/₄ full). Sprinkle each with about 2 teaspoons Streusel Topping. Bake 22 to 24 minutes or until golden brown. Immediately remove from pan. *12 muffins.*

STREUSEL TOPPING

2 tablespoons firm margarine or butter
¹/₄ cup all-purpose flour
2 tablespoons packed brown sugar
¹/₄ teaspoon ground cinnamon

Cut margarine into remaining ingredients in small bowl until crumbly.

JUMBO BLUEBERRY STREUSEL MUFFINS: Heat oven to 375°. Grease bottoms only of 4 jumbo muffin cups, 3¹/₂ × 1³/₄ inches. Divide batter and Streusel Topping evenly among muffin cups (cups will be almost full). Bake about 25 minutes, until toothpick inserted in center comes out clean. Let stand 5 minutes before removing from pan. *4 jumbo muffins.*

MINI BLUEBERRY STREUSEL MUFFINS: Grease bottoms only of 24 small muffin cups, 1³/₄ × 1 inch. Divide batter and Streusel Topping evenly among muffin cups (cups will be very full). Bake 12 to 14 minutes or until golden brown. Immediately remove from pan. *24 mini muffins.*

─────── ■ ───────

Banana-Blueberry Muffins

If you can't use up all of your ripe bananas, freeze them in their peels. When you're ready to bake with them, just thaw them and they'll be ready to use.

²/₃ cup milk
¹/₄ cup vegetable oil
¹/₂ cup mashed ripe banana (about 1 medium)
1 egg
2 cups all-purpose flour
²/₃ cup sugar
2¹/₂ teaspoons baking powder
¹/₂ teaspoon salt
¹/₄ teaspoon ground nutmeg
1 cup fresh or frozen (thawed and well drained) blueberries

Heat oven to 400°. Grease bottoms only of 12 medium muffin cups, 2¹/₂ × 1¹/₄ inches, or line with paper baking cups. Beat milk, oil, banana and egg in large bowl. Stir in remaining ingredients except blueberries just until flour is moistened. Fold in blueberries. Divide batter evenly among muffin cups (cups will be almost full). Sprinkle with sugar if desired. Bake 18 to 20 minutes or until golden brown. Immediately remove from pan. *12 muffins.*

Applesauce-Graham Muffins

If the raisins stick together, toss them with a little flour. You'll have a more even distribution of raisins throughout the muffin batter.

3/4 cup chunky applesauce
1/3 cup packed brown sugar
1/3 cup margarine or butter, melted
1 egg
1 cup all-purpose flour
2/3 cup graham cracker crumbs (about nine 2 1/2-inch squares)
2 teaspoons baking powder
1 teaspoon baking soda
1 teaspoon ground cinnamon
1 cup raisins

Heat oven to 400°. Grease bottoms only of 12 medium muffin cups, 2 1/2 × 1 1/4 inches, or line with paper baking cups. Beat applesauce, brown sugar, margarine and egg in large bowl. Stir in remaining ingredients except raisins just until flour is moistened. Fold in raisins. Divide batter evenly among muffin cups (cups will be almost full). Bake 18 to 20 minutes or until golden brown. Immediately remove from pan. *12 muffins.*

MINI APPLESAUCE-GRAHAM MUFFINS: Grease bottoms only of 24 small muffin cups, 1 3/4 × 1 inch. Divide batter evenly among muffin cups (cups will be very full). Bake 11 to 13 minutes or until golden brown. *24 mini muffins.*

Apple-Carrot Muffins

Streusel Topping (below)
1/4 cup milk
3 tablespoons vegetable oil
1 egg
1/2 cup all-purpose flour
1/2 cup whole wheat flour
1/3 cup sugar
1 1/2 teaspoons baking powder
1/4 teaspoon salt
1/4 teaspoon ground cinnamon
1/8 teaspoon ground cloves
1/2 cup shredded peeled or unpeeled apple (about 1 small)
1/2 cup shredded carrot (about 1 medium)
1/4 cup chopped walnuts, toasted if desired (see page 47)

Heat oven to 400°. Grease bottoms only of 6 medium muffin cups, 2 1/2 × 1 1/4 inches, or line with paper baking cups. Prepare Streusel Topping; reserve.

Beat milk, oil and egg in medium bowl. Stir in flours, sugar, baking powder, salt, cinnamon and cloves just until flour is moistened. Fold in apple, carrot and walnuts. Divide batter evenly among muffin cups (cups will be very full). Sprinkle with Streusel Topping. Bake 22 to 24 minutes or until golden brown. Immediately remove from pan. *6 muffins.*

STREUSEL TOPPING

1 tablespoon firm margarine or butter
2 tablespoons sugar
1 tablespoon all-purpose flour
1/8 teaspoon ground cinnamon

Cut margarine into remaining ingredients in small bowl until crumbly.

Tropical Banana Muffins

Chopping candied pineapple will be easier if you dip the knife into water before you begin.

1 cup mashed ripe bananas (about 2 medium)
¹⁄₂ cup packed brown sugar
¹⁄₃ cup milk
¹⁄₄ cup vegetable oil
1 egg
2 cups all-purpose flour
2¹⁄₂ teaspoons baking powder
¹⁄₂ teaspoon salt
¹⁄₂ cup chopped macadamia nuts or pecans
¹⁄₄ cup flaked coconut
¹⁄₄ cup chopped candied pineapple

Heat oven to 400°. Grease bottoms only of 12 medium muffin cups, 2¹⁄₂ × 1¹⁄₄ inches, or line with paper baking cups. Beat bananas, brown sugar, milk, oil and egg in large bowl. Stir in flour, baking powder and salt just until flour is moistened. Fold in macadamia nuts, coconut and pineapple. Divide batter evenly among muffin cups (cups will be very full). Bake 18 to 20 minutes or until golden brown. Immediately remove from pan. *12 muffins.*

Tropical Banana Muffins, Strawberry–Macadamia Nut Muffins (page 14)

Cranberry-Orange Muffins

You'll get about 1 tablespoon of grated orange peel from 1 medium orange.

1 cup milk
¹⁄₃ cup vegetable oil
1 tablespoon grated orange peel
1 egg
2 cups all-purpose flour
¹⁄₂ cup sugar
3 teaspoons baking powder
¹⁄₂ teaspoon salt
1 cup fresh or frozen cranberries, cut into halves, or sweetened dried cranberries

Heat oven to 400°. Grease bottoms only of 12 medium muffin cups, 2¹⁄₂ × 1¹⁄₄ inches, or line with paper baking cups. Beat milk, oil, orange peel and egg in large bowl. Stir in remaining ingredients except cranberries just until flour is moistened. Fold in cranberries. Divide batter evenly among muffin cups (cups will be about ³⁄₄ full). Sprinkle with sugar if desired. Bake 18 to 20 minutes or until golden brown. Immediately remove from pan. *12 muffins.*

Making the Perfect Muffin

Greasing

- Grease the bottoms only of muffin cups with shortening. Ungreased, the sides give the batter a surface to cling to as it bakes, resulting in muffins with nicely rounded tops. You can eliminate the greasing and make cleanup easier by using paper baking cups.
- Use shiny muffin pans for best browning. Even if you use dark nonstick muffin pans, grease the bottoms as directed. Dark pans absorb heat more readily than shiny pans, so with dark pans, better results are often achieved by reducing the oven temperature by 25°.

Mixing

- Mix the egg and other liquid ingredients with a fork until well blended. Occasionally, dry ingredients such as brown sugar or orange peel will be added at this point to ensure their even distribution throughout the batter.
- Stir in the dry ingredients just until the flour is moistened. The batter should be lumpy. Overmixed batter will result in tough muffins with peaked tops and an uneven texture.

Properly mixed muffin batter will be slightly lumpy. Fold in stir-ins just until they're evenly distributed.

Overmixed batter will result in peaked, tough muffins with large air holes. Properly mixed batter will yield tender muffins with rounded tops.

Folding

- If the recipe calls for folding in chopped nuts, pieces of fruit or other stir-ins, first sprinkle them over the batter. To fold, cut down through the center of the batter with a rubber spatula. Draw the spatula across the bottom and up the side of the bowl, folding the batter over the stir-ins on the top of the batter. Give the bowl a quarter turn and do it again. Repeat just until the stir-ins are distributed throughout the batter.

Baking

- Place the oven rack in the center of the oven for the best circulation of heat.
- Divide batter evenly among muffin cups, using a large spoon or ice-cream scoop. Wipe off any batter that spills onto the edge of the pan to avoid burning. Fill empty cups in the muffin pan half full of water to ensure even baking.
- Bake muffins for the minimum time specified in the recipe, then check for doneness. If necessary, bake a minute or two longer, then check them again.
- When muffins are done, immediately remove them from the muffin pan. Muffins left to cool in the pan will become soggy from trapped steam. If paper baking cups are used, muffins should lift out easily. Otherwise, loosen the muffins with a knife or metal spatula, then lift them out. Occasionally, a recipe will specify that muffins be left in the pan for a few minutes before removing; this allows fragile muffins to set up.

Reheating

- Muffins are best served warm. If they become too cool, heat uncovered in the microwave on medium (50%) just until warm—one muffin for 15 to 30 seconds, two muffins for 25 to 40 seconds, three muffins for 35 to 60 seconds and four muffins for 45 seconds to 1 minute 15 seconds.
- Or to reheat in a conventional oven, wrap muffins in aluminum foil and heat in a 400° oven about 5 minutes or until warm.

Toasted Oat–Date Muffins

1 cup quick-cooking or regular oats
³/₄ cup coarsely chopped walnuts
1 cup buttermilk
¹/₄ cup vegetable oil
2 tablespoons molasses
1 teaspoon vanilla
1 egg
1¹/₄ cups all-purpose flour
¹/₄ cup packed brown sugar
1¹/₂ teaspoons ground cinnamon
1 teaspoon baking soda
1 teaspoon baking powder
¹/₂ teaspoon salt
³/₄ cup chopped dates

Heat oven to 350°. Spread oats and walnuts in ungreased rectangular pan, 13 × 9 × 2 inches. Bake 15 to 20 minutes, stirring occasionally, until light brown; cool.

Heat oven to 400°. Grease bottoms only of 12 medium muffin cups, 2¹/₂ × 1¹/₄ inches, or line with paper baking cups. Beat buttermilk, oil, molasses, vanilla and egg in large bowl. Stir in oats, walnuts and remaining ingredients except dates just until flour is moistened. Fold in dates. Divide batter evenly among muffin cups (cups will be almost full). Bake 18 to 20 minutes or until toothpick inserted in center comes out clean. Immediately remove from pan. *12 muffins.*

Raspberry-filled Chocolate Chip Muffins

1 cup milk
¹/₃ cup vegetable oil
1 egg
2 cups all-purpose flour
¹/₂ cup sugar
2 teaspoons baking powder
¹/₂ teaspoon salt
¹/₂ cup miniature semisweet chocolate chips
¹/₄ cup raspberry jam or preserves

Heat oven to 400°. Grease bottoms only of 12 medium muffin cups, 2¹/₂ × 1¹/₄ inches, or line with paper baking cups. Beat milk, oil and egg in large bowl. Stir in flour, sugar, baking powder and salt just until flour is moistened. Fold in chocolate chips. Fill muffin cups ¹/₃ full. Place about 1 teaspoon jam on batter in each muffin cup. Top with remaining batter. Sprinkle with sugar if desired. Bake 18 to 20 minutes or until golden brown. Immediately remove from pan. *12 muffins.*

BAKERY-STYLE RASPBERRY-FILLED CHOCOLATE CHIP MUFFINS: Grease bottoms only of 10 medium muffin cups, 2¹/₂ × 1¹/₄ inches, or line with paper baking cups. Fill muffin cups about ¹/₂ full. Place about 1¹/₂ teaspoons jam on batter in each muffin cup. Top with remaining batter. Bake 22 to 24 minutes or until golden brown. *10 muffins.*

Raspberry-filled Chocolate Chip Muffins, Chocolate-Toffee Muffins (page 10)

Chocolate-Toffee Muffins

1¼ cups milk
⅓ cup vegetable oil
1 egg
2 cups all-purpose flour
⅔ cup sugar
⅓ cup cocoa
2 teaspoons baking powder
½ teaspoon salt
3 bars (1.4 ounces each) chocolate-covered English toffee candy, chopped, or ¾ cup toffee chips or ½ cup almond brickle chips and ¼ cup miniature semisweet chocolate chips

Heat oven to 400°. Grease bottoms only of 12 medium muffin cups, 2½ × 1¼ inches, or line with paper baking cups. Beat milk, oil and egg in large bowl. Stir in remaining ingredients except candy just until flour is moistened. Fold in candy. Divide batter evenly among muffin cups (cups will be full). Bake 18 to 20 minutes or until toothpick inserted in center comes out clean. Immediately remove from pan. *12 muffins.*

Mocha Muffins

It's easy to freeze these muffins and reheat them later. Wrap cooled muffins in freezer-proof material and freeze up to 3 months. To reheat them, microwave uncovered on medium (50%) 1 to 1 minute 30 seconds for 2 muffins, or 1 minute 30 seconds to 3 minutes for 4 muffins.

⅓ cup packed brown sugar
1 cup milk
⅓ cup vegetable oil
1 tablespoon freeze-dried or powdered instant coffee (dry)
1 egg
2 cups all-purpose flour
2 tablespoons cocoa
2½ teaspoons baking powder
½ teaspoon salt
1 cup semisweet chocolate chunks or chips

Heat oven to 400°. Grease bottoms only of 12 medium muffin cups, 2½ × 1¼ inches, or line with paper baking cups. Beat brown sugar, milk, oil, coffee granules and egg in large bowl.

Mix flour, cocoa, baking powder and salt; stir into milk mixture just until flour is moistened. Fold in chocolate chunks. Divide batter evenly among muffin cups (cups will be almost full). Bake 18 to 20 minutes or until toothpick inserted in center comes out clean. Immediately remove from pan. *12 muffins.*

Pear-Fig Muffins

Just about any dried fruit will be delicious in this recipe. Try substituting raisins, prunes, dates or a dried fruit mixture for the figs.

3/4 cup milk
1/3 cup vegetable oil
1 egg
1 3/4 cups all-purpose flour
1/3 cup sugar
2 1/2 teaspoons baking powder
1/2 teaspoon salt
1/4 teaspoon ground nutmeg
1 cup chopped unpeeled pear (about 1 medium)
1/2 cup chopped dried figs

Heat oven to 400°. Grease bottoms only of 12 medium muffin cups, 2 1/2 × 1 1/4 inches, or line with paper baking cups. Beat milk, oil and egg in large bowl. Stir in remaining ingredients except pear and figs just until flour is moistened. Fold in pear and figs. Divide batter evenly among muffin cups (cups will be almost full). Sprinkle with sugar if desired. Bake 18 to 20 minutes or until golden brown. Immediately remove from pan. *12 muffins.*

BAKERY-STYLE PEAR-FIG MUFFINS: Grease bottoms only of 10 medium muffin cups, 2 1/2 × 1 1/4 inches, or line with paper baking cups. Divide batter evenly among muffin cups (cups will be very full). Bake 22 to 24 minutes or until golden brown. *10 muffins.*

Praline-Peach Muffins

Topping (below)
1/2 cup packed brown sugar
1/2 cup milk
1/3 cup vegetable oil
1 teaspoon vanilla
1 egg
1 2/3 cups all-purpose flour
2 teaspoons baking powder
1/4 teaspoon salt
1 cup chopped fresh, frozen (thawed and drained) or canned (well-drained) peaches
1/2 cup coarsely chopped pecans

Heat oven to 400°. Grease bottoms only of 12 medium muffin cups, 2 1/2 × 1 1/4 inches, or line with paper baking cups. Prepare Topping; reserve.

Beat brown sugar, milk, oil, vanilla and egg in large bowl. Stir in flour, baking powder and salt just until flour is moistened. Fold in peaches and pecans. Divide batter evenly among muffin cups (cups will be almost full). Sprinkle with Topping.

Bake 18 to 20 minutes or until golden brown. Immediately remove from pan. *12 muffins.*

TOPPING

1 tablespoon firm margarine or butter
1/4 cup packed brown sugar
1/4 cup chopped pecans

Cut margarine into remaining ingredients in small bowl until crumbly.

Apricot-Ginger Muffins

Crystallized ginger is made by cooking pieces of gingerroot in a sugar syrup and then coating them with coarse sugar. Look for crystallized ginger in the spice section of your supermarket.

> 1 cup plain yogurt
> 1/3 cup vegetable oil
> 2 tablespoons finely chopped crystallized ginger
> 1 egg
> 2 cups all-purpose flour
> 1/2 cup sugar
> 2 teaspoons baking powder
> 1 teaspoon baking soda
> 1/2 cup chopped dried apricots

Heat oven to 400°. Grease bottoms only of 12 medium muffin cups, 2 1/2 × 1 1/4 inches, or line with paper baking cups. Beat yogurt, oil, ginger and egg in large bowl. Stir in remaining ingredients except apricots just until flour is moistened. Fold in apricots. Divide batter evenly among muffin cups (cups will be very full). Sprinkle with sugar if desired. Bake 16 to 18 minutes or until golden brown. Immediately remove from pan. *12 muffins.*

Maraschino Cherry Muffins

> 1/4 cup sugar
> 1/4 cup (1/2 stick) margarine or butter, melted
> 1/2 cup milk
> 1 egg
> 1 cup all-purpose flour
> 1 teaspoon baking powder
> 1/4 teaspoon salt
> 1/3 cup chopped maraschino cherries, drained and 4 teaspoons juice, reserved
> 1/4 cup chopped blanched almonds
> Glaze (below)

Heat oven to 400°. Grease bottoms only of 6 medium muffin cups, 2 1/2 × 1 1/4 inches, or line with paper baking cups. Beat sugar, margarine, milk and egg in medium bowl. Stir in flour, baking powder and salt just until flour is moistened. Fold in cherries and almonds. Divide batter evenly among muffin cups (cups will be full). Bake 20 to 22 minutes or until golden brown. Immediately remove from pan. Drizzle Glaze over warm muffins. *6 muffins.*

GLAZE

> 1/2 cup powdered sugar
> 3 to 4 teaspoons maraschino cherry juice

Mix ingredients until smooth and drizzling consistency.

MINI MARASCHINO CHERRY MUFFINS: Grease bottoms only of 18 small muffin cups, 1 3/4 × 1 inch. Divide batter evenly among muffin cups (cups will be very full). Bake 13 to 15 minutes or until golden brown. *18 mini muffins.*

Mini, Bakery-Style and Jumbo Muffins

Convert your favorite 12-muffin recipe to mini, bakery-style or jumbo muffins using the chart and tips below.

Muffin Size	Muffin Cup Size	Oven Temperature	Baking Time	Yield
Mini	1¾ × 1 inch (small)	400°	10 to 17 minutes	24
Bakery-style	2½ × 1¼ inches (medium)	400°	20 to 26 minutes	8 to 10
Jumbo	3½ × 1¾ inches (large)	375°	25 to 35 minutes	4

Success Tips:

- This chart offers *general* guidelines for converting regular-size muffins to mini, bakery-style or jumbo muffins. When you determine the best baking times for your favorite muffin recipes, be sure to write them down for future use.
- Because there is a wide range in baking times, check for doneness at the minimum time. If necessary, bake longer, checking every minute or two, until done.
- When making bakery-style muffins with softer, more liquid batters, make 10 muffins. Stiffer, thicker batters can be used to make 8 bakery-style muffins.
- Muffin batters with large pieces of nuts, fruit or chocolate work better as bakery-style or jumbo muffins because the stir-ins are too large for mini muffins.
- Muffin batters that are very rich work well as mini muffins; a larger muffin may be too much for one serving.

Strawberry–Macadamia Nut Muffins

Macadamia nuts have a rich, buttery, slightly sweet flavor. To keep them fresh, store opened containers of macadamia nuts in the refrigerator or freezer. If you'd like, you can substitute chopped pecans or almonds for the macadamia nuts in this recipe.

> *³/₄ cup milk*
> *¹/₃ cup margarine or butter, melted*
> *1 egg*
> *2 cups all-purpose flour*
> *²/₃ cup sugar*
> *2 teaspoons baking powder*
> *¹/₂ teaspoon salt*
> *1 cup chopped fresh strawberries*
> *¹/₂ cup chopped macadamia nuts*

Heat oven to 400°. Grease bottoms only of 12 medium muffin cups, 2¹/₂ × 1¹/₄ inches, or line with paper baking cups. Beat milk, margarine and egg in large bowl. Stir in flour, sugar, baking powder and salt just until flour is moistened. Fold in strawberries and macadamia nuts. Divide batter evenly among muffin cups (cups will be almost full). Sprinkle with sugar if desired. Bake 20 to 22 minutes or until golden brown. Immediately remove from pan. *12 muffins.*

Gingerbread Muffins

Serve Lemon–Cream Cheese Spread (page 85) with these muffins—it'll be a sure-fire hit!

> *¹/₄ cup packed brown sugar*
> *¹/₂ cup dark molasses*
> *¹/₃ cup milk*
> *¹/₃ cup vegetable oil*
> *1 egg*
> *2 cups all-purpose flour*
> *1 teaspoon baking powder*
> *1 teaspoon ground ginger*
> *¹/₂ teaspoon salt*
> *¹/₂ teaspoon baking soda*
> *¹/₂ teaspoon ground cinnamon*
> *¹/₄ teaspoon ground allspice*

Heat oven to 400°. Grease bottoms only of 12 medium muffin cups, 2¹/₂ × 1¹/₄ inches, or line with paper baking cups. Beat brown sugar, molasses, milk, oil and egg in large bowl. Stir in remaining ingredients just until flour is moistened. Divide batter evenly among muffin cups (cups will be about ³/₄ full). Bake 18 to 20 minutes or until toothpick inserted in center comes out clean. Immediately remove from pan. *12 muffins.*

BAKERY–STYLE GINGERBREAD MUFFINS: Grease bottoms only of 10 medium muffin cups, 2¹/₂ × 1¹/₄ inches, or line with paper baking cups. Divide batter evenly among muffin cups (cups will be almost full). Bake 20 to 22 minutes or until toothpick inserted in center comes out clean. *10 muffins.*

Spiced Honey-Lemon Muffins

Some of the warm glaze will drip off the warm muffins, so place muffins on a serving plate, cookie sheet or waxed paper for easier cleanup.

3/4 cup milk
1/3 cup vegetable oil
1/4 cup honey
2 teaspoons grated lemon peel
1 egg
2 cups all-purpose flour
2 1/2 teaspoons baking powder
1/2 teaspoon salt
1/2 teaspoon ground cinnamon
1/4 teaspoon ground allspice
Honey-Lemon Glaze (right)

Heat oven to 400°. Grease bottoms only of 8 medium muffin cups, 2 1/2 × 1 1/4 inches, or line with paper baking cups. Beat milk, oil, honey, lemon peel and egg in large bowl. Stir in remaining ingredients except Honey-Lemon Glaze just until flour is moistened. Divide batter evenly among muffin cups (cups will be about 3/4 full). Bake 20 to 22 minutes or until golden brown. Immediately remove from pan. Brush Honey-Lemon Glaze over warm muffins. *8 muffins.*

HONEY-LEMON GLAZE

2 tablespoons honey
1/4 teaspoon grated lemon peel
2 teaspoons lemon juice

Mix all ingredients until well blended.

BAKERY–STYLE SPICED HONEY-LEMON MUFFINS: Grease bottoms only of 6 medium muffin cups, 2 1/2 × 1 1/4 inches, or line with paper baking cups. Divide batter evenly among muffin cups (cups will be very full). Bake 22 to 24 minutes or until golden brown. *6 muffins.*

Peanut Butter–Honey Muffins

1 cup milk
1/2 cup honey
1/3 cup peanut butter
1 egg
2 cups all-purpose flour
2 teaspoons baking powder
1/2 teaspoon salt
1/2 cup chopped peanuts

Heat oven to 400°. Grease bottoms only of 12 medium muffin cups, 2½ × 1¼ inches, or line with paper baking cups. Beat milk, honey, peanut butter and egg in large bowl with wire whisk. Stir in flour, baking powder and salt with spoon just until flour is moistened. Fold in peanuts. Divide batter evenly among muffin cups (cups will be about ¾ full). Bake 18 to 20 minutes or until golden brown. Immediately remove from pan. 12 muffins.

MINI PEANUT BUTTER–HONEY MUFFINS: Grease bottoms only of 24 small muffin cups, 1¾ × 1 inch. Divide batter evenly among muffin cups (cups will be very full). Bake 15 to 17 minutes or until golden brown. *24 mini muffins.*

Cream Cheese–filled Pumpkin Muffins

You can use the leftover pumpkin in Pumpkin Bread (page 71) or Pumpkin-Fruit Bread (page 109).

Cream Cheese Filling (below)
1/2 cup canned pumpkin
1/3 cup packed brown sugar
1/2 cup milk
1/4 cup vegetable oil
2 eggs
1½ cups all-purpose flour
2½ teaspoons baking powder
1 teaspoon ground cinnamon
1/2 teaspoon salt
1/2 teaspoon ground cloves
1/2 cup chopped walnuts or pecans

Heat oven to 400°. Grease bottoms only of 12 medium muffin cups, 2½ × 1¼ inches, or line with paper baking cups. Prepare Cream Cheese Filling; reserve.

Beat pumpkin, brown sugar, milk, oil and eggs in large bowl. Stir in remaining ingredients except walnuts just until flour is moistened. Fold in walnuts. Fill muffin cups ⅓ full. Place about 1 rounded teaspoon filling on batter in each muffin cup. Top with remaining batter. Bake 20 to 22 minutes or until golden brown. Immediately remove from pan. *12 muffins.*

CREAM CHEESE FILLING

1 package (3 ounces) cream cheese, softened
1 tablespoon granulated sugar
1 tablespoon milk

Mix all ingredients until smooth.

Cream Cheese–filled Pumpkin Muffins, Cranberry-Orange Muffins (page 5)

Lemon Yogurt–Poppy Seed Muffins

$1/3$ cup milk
$1/4$ cup vegetable oil
1 container (6 ounces) lemon yogurt
  ($2/3$ cup)
1 egg
$1^3/4$ cups all-purpose flour
$1/4$ cup sugar
2 tablespoons poppy seeds
1 tablespoon grated lemon peel
$2^1/2$ teaspoons baking powder
$1/2$ teaspoon baking soda
$1/2$ teaspoon salt
Lemon Glaze (below)

Heat oven to 400°. Grease bottoms only of 12 medium muffin cups, $2^1/2$ × $1^1/4$ inches, or line with paper baking cups. Beat milk, oil, yogurt and egg in large bowl. Stir in remaining ingredients except Lemon Glaze just until flour is moistened. Divide batter evenly among muffin cups (cups will be about 3/4 full). Bake 16 to 18 minutes or until golden brown. Immediately remove from pan. Drizzle Lemon Glaze over warm muffins. 12 muffins.

LEMON GLAZE

$1/2$ cup powdered sugar
2 to 3 teaspoons lemon juice

Mix ingredients until smooth and drizzling consistency.

MINI LEMON YOGURT—POPPY SEED MUFFINS: Grease bottoms only of 24 small muffin cups, $1^3/4$ × 1 inch. Divide batter evenly among muffin cups (cups will be very full). Bake 10 to 12 minutes or until golden brown. *24 mini muffins.*

Refrigerator Bran Muffins

These muffins are delicious and convenient whether you want to make them right away or refrigerate the batter and make freshly baked muffins up to 4 days later.

1 egg
2 tablespoons milk†
$1^2/3$ cups Bran Muffin Batter (below)

Heat oven to 400°. Grease bottoms only of 6 medium muffin cups, $2^1/2$ × $1^1/4$ inches, or line with paper baking cups. Beat egg and milk in medium bowl; add Bran Muffin Batter (batter will be stiff). Break up batter with fork; gently mix just until blended. Divide batter evenly among muffin cups (cups will be about 3/4 full). Bake 20 to 22 minutes or until golden brown. Immediately remove from pan. *6 muffins.*

BRAN MUFFIN BATTER

1 cup packed brown sugar
$1^1/2$ cups buttermilk
$3/4$ cup vegetable oil
$1^1/2$ cups finely crushed bran cereal
  shreds (about $2^1/2$ cups uncrushed)
2 cups all-purpose flour
$1^1/2$ teaspoons baking soda
$1/2$ teaspoon salt
$3/4$ cup raisins

Mix brown sugar, buttermilk and oil in large sins just until flour is moistened. Fold in raisins. Cover and refrigerate up to 4 days. *Enough batter for 18 muffins.*

†Batter can be used before refrigerating. Prepare as directed—except omit milk.

Marzipan Muffins

You'll find the marzipan easier to chop if you freeze it for 1 or 2 hours until it's firm.

1¼ cups sour cream
¼ cup vegetable oil
1 egg
1¾ cups all-purpose flour
½ cup sugar
2 teaspoons baking powder
½ teaspoon baking soda
½ teaspoon salt
½ teaspoon ground cardamom
½ package (7- to 8.8-ounce size) marzipan or almond paste, chopped

Heat oven to 400°. Grease bottoms only of 12 medium muffin cups, 2½ × 1¼ inches, or line with paper baking cups. Beat sour cream, oil and egg in large bowl. Stir in remaining ingredients except marzipan just until flour is moistened. Fold in marzipan. Divide batter evenly among muffin cups (cups will be almost full). Bake 18 to 20 minutes or until golden brown. Immediately remove from pan. *12 muffins.*

Double Corn Muffins

Frozen whole-kernel corn (thawed), canned whole-kernel corn (drained) or leftover cooked corn will all be delicious in this recipe.

⅔ cup milk
3 tablespoons vegetable oil
1 egg
¾ cup all-purpose flour
¾ cup yellow cornmeal
2 tablespoons sugar
1 teaspoon baking powder
½ teaspoon salt
1 cup cooked whole kernel corn

Heat oven to 400°. Grease bottoms only of 8 medium muffin cups, 2½ × 1¼ inches, or line with paper baking cups. Beat milk, oil and egg in medium bowl. Stir in remaining ingredients except corn just until flour is moistened. Fold in corn. Divide batter evenly among muffin cups (cups will be about ¾ full). Bake 18 to 20 minutes or until golden brown. Immediately remove from pan. *8 muffins.*

Quick Muffins

Delicious muffins are a breeze when you start with convenient Bisquick® Original baking mix. Just choose your favorite flavor combinations from the chart below, and follow these simple instructions. You'll be enjoying fresh-from-the-oven muffins in no time!

Heat oven to 400°. Grease bottoms only of 12 medium muffin cups, $2\frac{1}{2} \times 1\frac{1}{4}$ inches, or line with paper baking cups. Beat wet ingredients in a large bowl. Stir in dry ingredients just until baking mix is moistened. Fold in additional ingredients. Divide batter evenly among muffin cups. Bake 15 to 20 minutes or until golden brown. Immediately remove from pan. *12 muffins.*

Muffins	Wet Ingredients	Dry Ingredients	Additional Ingredients
Banana	1¼ cups mashed bananas (about 3 medium) 3 tablespoons vegetable oil 1 egg	2 cups Bisquick ⅓ cup sugar	¾ cup fresh or frozen (thawed) blueberries OR 1 cup chocolate-covered peanuts OR ½ cup flaked coconut OR ¾ cup chopped nuts
Corn	⅔ cup milk 2 tablespoons vegetable oil 1 egg	1½ cups Bisquick ¾ cup yellow cornmeal	6 strips bacon, crisply cooked and crumbled OR ½ cup shredded Cheddar cheese OR 1 can (4 ounces) chopped green chilies, drained OR 1 cup canned whole kernel corn, drained
Honey	⅔ cup milk ¼ cup honey 2 tablespoons vegetable oil 1 egg	2 cups Bisquick ½ teaspoon ground nutmeg	½ cup granola OR ¾ cup chopped almonds OR ½ cup chopped dates OR 2 tablespoons finely chopped crystallized ginger

Muffins	Wet Ingredients	Dry Ingredients	Additional Ingredients

Oatmeal	²/₃ cup milk
	2 tablespoons
	  vegetable oil
	1 egg
		1½ cups Bisquick
		¾ cup quick-
		  cooking oats
		⅓ cup sugar
		1 teaspoon ground
		  cinnamon
			¾ cup chopped apple
			OR
			¾ cup butterscotch-flavored chips
			OR
			½ cup raisins
			OR
			½ cup roasted sunflower nuts

Orange	²/₃ cup orange
	  juice
	2 tablespoons
	  vegetable oil
	1 teaspoon
	  grated
	  orange peel
	1 egg
		2 cups Bisquick
		2 tablespoons
		  sugar
			½ cup semisweet chocolate chips
			OR
			¾ cup chopped fresh or frozen
			  cranberries
			OR
			¾ cup chopped candied
			  pineapple
			OR
			1 tablespoon poppy seed

Sour
Cream
	½ cup sour
	  cream
	2 eggs
		1½ cups Bisquick
		¼ teaspoon onion
		  powder
			1 cup shredded Cheddar cheese
			OR
			1 tablespoon chopped fresh or
			  1 teaspoon dried dill weed
			OR
			1 cup finely chopped fully cooked
			  smoked ham
			OR
			½ cup sliced ripe or pimiento-
			  stuffed olives

Fresh Herb–Yogurt Muffins

1 cup plain yogurt
¹/₃ cup olive or vegetable oil
2 tablespoons chopped fresh or 2 teaspoons dried basil, oregano or rosemary leaves
1 egg
2 cups all-purpose flour
2 teaspoons baking powder
¹/₂ teaspoon baking soda
¹/₂ teaspoon salt

Heat oven to 400°. Grease bottoms only of 12 medium muffin cups, 2¹/₂ × 1¹/₄ inches, or line with paper baking cups. Beat yogurt, oil, basil and egg in large bowl. Stir in remaining ingredients just until flour is moistened. Divide batter evenly among muffin cups (cups will be about ³/₄ full). Bake 18 to 20 minutes or until golden brown. Immediately remove from pan. *12 muffins*.

BAKERY-STYLE FRESH HERB–YOGURT MUFFINS: Grease bottoms only of 8 medium muffin cups, 2¹/₂ × 1¹/₄ inches, or line with paper baking cups. Divide batter evenly among muffin cups (cups will be very full). Bake 20 to 22 minutes or until golden brown. *8 muffins*.

Garlic and Chive Muffins

You can experiment with the amount of garlic in this recipe. If you want a milder garlic flavor, just use a little less.

1 cup sour cream
¹/₂ cup milk
¹/₄ cup (¹/₂ stick) margarine or butter, melted
2 tablespoons chopped fresh or freeze-dried chives
1 clove garlic, finely chopped (about ¹/₂ teaspoon)
1 egg
2 cups all-purpose flour
2 teaspoons baking powder
¹/₂ teaspoon baking soda
¹/₂ teaspoon salt

Heat oven to 400°. Grease bottoms only of 12 medium muffin cups, 2¹/₂ × 1¹/₄ inches, or line with paper baking cups. Beat sour cream, milk, margarine, chives, garlic and egg in large bowl. Stir in remaining ingredients just until flour is moistened. Divide batter evenly among muffin cups (cups will be almost full). Sprinkle with coarse salt if desired. Bake 18 to 20 minutes or until golden brown. Immediately remove from pan. *12 muffins*.

Cottage Cheese–Dill Muffins

*³/₄ cup small curd creamed cottage
 cheese*
³/₄ cup milk
*¹/₄ cup (¹/₂ stick) margarine or butter,
 melted*
*1 tablespoon chopped fresh or 1 tea-
 spoon dried dill weed*
1 egg
2 cups all-purpose flour
2 tablespoons grated Parmesan cheese
2¹/₂ teaspoons baking powder

Heat oven to 400°. Grease bottoms only of 12 medium muffin cups, 2¹/₂ × 1¹/₄ inches, or line with paper baking cups. Beat cottage cheese, milk, margarine, dill weed and egg in large bowl. Stir in remaining ingredients just until flour is moistened. Divide batter evenly among muffin cups (cups will be almost full). Sprinkle with additional grated Parmesan cheese if desired. Bake 18 to 20 minutes or until golden brown. Immediately remove from pan. *12 muffins.*

BAKERY-STYLE COTTAGE CHEESE–DILL MUFFINS: Grease bottoms only of 8 medium muffin cups, 2¹/₂ × 1¹/₄ inches, or line with paper baking cups. Divide batter evenly among muffin cups (cups will be very full). Bake 23 to 25 minutes or until golden brown. *8 muffins.*

Blue Cheese and Mushroom Muffins

*1 cup coarsely chopped fresh
 mushrooms*
2 tablespoons chopped green onions
*1 clove garlic, finely chopped (about
 ¹/₂ teaspoon)*
¹/₃ cup margarine or butter
1¹/₄ cups milk
¹/₄ cup crumbled blue cheese
1 egg
2 cups all-purpose flour
3 teaspoons baking powder
¹/₄ teaspoon salt
¹/₈ teaspoon pepper
¹/₄ cup finely chopped walnuts

Heat oven to 400°. Grease bottoms only of 12 medium muffin cups, 2¹/₂ × 1¹/₄ inches, or line with paper baking cups. Cook mushrooms, green onions and garlic in margarine in 10-inch skillet over medium heat 6 to 8 minutes, stirring frequently, until mushrooms are tender; cool slightly.

Beat milk, blue cheese, egg and mushroom mixture in large bowl. Stir in flour, baking powder, salt and pepper just until flour is moistened. Divide batter evenly among muffin cups (cups will be about ³/₄ full). Sprinkle with walnuts. Bake 18 to 20 minutes or until light golden brown. Immediately remove from pan. *12 muffins.*

Cheese and Spinach Muffins

1¼ cups milk
⅓ cup margarine or butter, melted
1 egg
2 cups all-purpose flour
¼ cup grated Parmesan cheese
2 tablespoons chopped green onions
3 teaspoons baking powder
¼ teaspoon salt
½ cup coarsely chopped fresh or ¼ cup very well drained, frozen (thawed) chopped spinach
½ cup shredded Swiss cheese
Grated Parmesan cheese

Heat oven to 400°. Grease bottoms only of 12 medium muffin cups, 2½ × 1¼ inches, or line with paper baking cups. Beat milk, margarine and egg in large bowl. Stir in flour, ¼ cup Parmesan cheese, the green onions, baking powder and salt just until flour is moistened. Fold in spinach and Swiss cheese. Divide batter evenly among muffin cups (cups will be almost full). Sprinkle with Parmesan cheese. Bake 18 to 20 minutes or until golden brown. Immediately remove from pan. *12 muffins.*

JUMBO CHEESE AND SPINACH MUFFINS: Heat oven to 375°. Grease bottoms only of 4 jumbo muffin cups, 3½ × 1¾ inches. Divide batter evenly among muffin cups (cups will be almost full). Bake 30 to 35 minutes or until toothpick inserted in center comes out clean. Let stand 5 minutes before removing from pan. *4 jumbo muffins.*

Parmesan-Tomato Muffins

1 cup milk
¼ cup vegetable oil
1 egg
2 cups all-purpose flour
¼ cup grated Parmesan cheese
1 tablespoon chopped fresh or 1 teaspoon dried basil leaves
2½ teaspoons baking powder
¼ teaspoon salt
½ cup chopped sun-dried tomatoes in olive oil, drained
¼ cup chopped pimiento-stuffed olives
Grated Parmesan cheese

Heat oven to 400°. Grease bottoms only of 12 medium muffin cups, 2½ × 1¼ inches, or line with paper baking cups. Beat milk, oil and egg in large bowl. Stir in flour, ¼ cup Parmesan cheese, the basil, baking powder and salt just until flour is moistened. Fold in tomatoes and olives. Divide batter evenly among muffin cups (cups will be almost full). Sprinkle with Parmesan cheese. Bake 18 to 20 minutes or until golden brown. Immediately remove from pan. *12 muffins.*

JUMBO PARMESAN-TOMATO MUFFINS: Heat oven to 375°. Grease bottoms only of 4 jumbo muffin cups, 3½ × 1¾ inches. Divide batter evenly among muffin cups (cups will be almost full). Bake 30 to 35 minutes or until toothpick inserted in center comes out clean. Let stand 5 minutes before removing from pan. *4 jumbo muffins.*

Cheese and Spinach Muffins, Wild Rice–Sausage Muffins (page 27)

Olive–Cream Cheese Muffins

*2 packages (3 ounces each) cream
  cheese, softened*
1 egg
1 cup milk
1/4 cup vegetable oil
2 cups all-purpose flour
2 1/2 teaspoons baking powder
1/4 teaspoon salt
1/2 cup sliced pimiento-stuffed olives

Heat oven to 400°. Grease bottoms only of 12 medium muffin cups, 2 1/2 × 1 1/4 inches, or line with paper baking cups. Beat cream cheese and egg in large bowl until almost smooth. Gradually stir in milk and oil. Stir in flour, baking powder and salt just until flour is moistened. Fold in olives. Divide batter evenly among muffin cups (cups will be almost full). Bake 18 to 20 minutes or until light golden brown. Immediately remove from pan. *12 muffins.*

BAKERY-STYLE OLIVE–CREAM CHEESE MUFFINS: Grease bottoms only of 8 medium muffin cups, 2 1/2 × 1 1/4 inches, or line with paper baking cups. Divide batter evenly among muffin cups (cups will be very full). Bake 22 to 24 minutes or until light golden brown. *8 muffins.*

Ham-Dijon Muffins

For a change of pace, try other mustards such as spicy brown or stone-ground in this recipe.

1 cup milk
1/3 cup vegetable oil
*2 tablespoons country-style Dijon
  mustard*
1 egg
2 cups all-purpose flour
2 1/2 teaspoons baking powder
1/4 teaspoon salt
*3/4 cup chopped fully cooked smoked
  ham (about 1/4 pound)*

Heat oven to 400°. Grease bottoms only of 12 medium muffin cups, 2 1/2 × 1 1/4 inches, or line with paper baking cups. Beat milk, oil, mustard and egg in large bowl. Stir in flour, baking powder and salt just until flour is moistened. Fold in ham. Divide batter evenly among muffin cups (cups will be almost full). Bake 18 to 20 minutes or until light golden brown. Immediately remove from pan. Refrigerate any remaining muffins. *12 muffins.*

BAKERY-STYLE HAM-DIJON MUFFINS: Grease bottoms only of 8 medium muffin cups, 2 1/2 × 1 1/4 inches, or line with paper baking cups. Divide batter evenly among muffin cups (cups will be very full). Bake 22 to 24 minutes or until light golden brown. *8 muffins.*

Wild Rice–Sausage Muffins

To make ¾ cup cooked wild rice, heat ½ cup rinsed uncooked wild rice, ⅔ cup water and a dash of salt, if desired, to boiling in a heavy saucepan, stirring once or twice. Reduce heat, cover and simmer 40 to 50 minutes or until tender.

¼ pound bulk pork sausage
¼ cup sliced green onions
Vegetable oil
1 cup milk
1 egg
2 cups all-purpose flour
3 teaspoons baking powder
½ teaspoon salt
¼ teaspoon pepper
¾ cup cooked wild rice

Heat oven to 400°. Grease bottoms only of 12 medium muffin cups, 2½ × 1¼ inches, or line with paper baking cups. Cook sausage and green onions in 10-inch skillet over medium heat, stirring frequently, until sausage is brown. Drain if necessary, reserving fat. Cool sausage slightly; crumble.

Measure reserved fat and enough oil to measure ⅓ cup. Beat sausage mixture, oil mixture, milk and egg in large bowl. Stir in flour, baking powder, salt and pepper just until flour is moistened. Fold in wild rice. Divide batter evenly among muffin cups (cups will be about ¾ full). Bake 18 to 20 minutes or until golden brown. Immediately remove from pan. Refrigerate any remaining muffins. *12 muffins.*

BAKERY-STYLE WILD RICE–SAUSAGE MUF-FINS: Grease bottoms only of 8 medium muffin cups, 2½ × 1¼ inches, or line with paper baking cups. Divide batter evenly among muffin cups (cups will be very full). Bake 22 to 24 minutes or until golden brown. *8 muffins.*

Bacon and Cheddar Muffins

The seeds and membranes inside chili peppers are the hottest parts, so if you don't remove them before chopping the jalapeño chili, expect your muffins to be extra hot!

1¼ cups milk
¼ cup vegetable oil
1 jalapeño chili, seeded and chopped
1 egg
2 cups all-purpose flour
3 teaspoons baking powder
¼ teaspoon salt
1 cup shredded Cheddar cheese (4 ounces)
6 slices bacon, crisply cooked and crumbled

Heat oven to 400°. Grease bottoms only of 12 medium muffin cups, 2½ × 1¼ inches, or line with paper baking cups. Beat milk, oil, chili and egg in large bowl. Stir in flour, baking powder and salt just until flour is moistened. Fold in cheese and bacon. Divide batter evenly among muffin cups (cups will be about ¾ full). Bake 18 to 20 minutes or until golden brown. Immediately remove from pan. Refrigerate any remaining muffins. *12 muffins.*

2
Favorite Biscuits and Scones

Put some hot biscuits, spicy sausage, fluffy eggs and home-fried potatoes on a plate, and you have a good old-fashioned breakfast fit for a king. From coffee shops and diners, to southern breakfast nooks and the Western frontier, there's something downright American about biscuits. True to our roots, we've included such old-time family favorites as Buttermilk Biscuits and Country-style Butter Biscuits in this book—and they're just as delicious as ever. You'll also find terrific new recipes here, such as Orange–Chocolate Chip Biscuits and Pesto Biscuits . . . they'll go like hotcakes!

If you've never tried a scone, now's the time to do it. You may be wondering what a scone is—it's actually a little hard to describe. There are no clear-cut definitions that distinguish scones from biscuits. In this book, our scone recipes contain egg and whipping cream or half-and-half to make them richer than biscuits. Often, the scones are somewhat sweeter than the biscuits. Our biscuits and scones differ in shape, too. Most of the biscuits are cut into rounds, and the scones are cut into wedges or diamonds. (It is quite common to see round scones, so don't be surprised if you're ever served a biscuit-shaped scone.) The English serve scones at afternoon tea with clotted cream (a rich, thickened cream) and jam. Experiment and see how you like them best. You might want to host an afternoon tea party to try a variety of recipes. But we think you'll agree that Coconut-Pecan Scones and Apricot–White Chocolate Scones, for example, will be absolutely appropriate any time of day.

Basil-Pepper Biscuits (page 34)

Buttermilk Biscuits

If you don't have buttermilk on hand, mix 2¼ teaspoons vinegar and enough milk to make ¾ cup. Let the mixture stand a few minutes until slightly thickened.

> ½ cup shortening
> 2 cups all-purpose flour
> 1 tablespoon sugar
> 2 teaspoons baking powder
> 1 teaspoon salt
> ¼ teaspoon baking soda
> About ¾ cup buttermilk

Heat oven to 450°. Cut shortening into flour, sugar, baking powder, salt and baking soda with pastry blender in large bowl until mixture resembles fine crumbs. Stir in just enough buttermilk so dough leaves side of bowl and forms a ball.

Turn dough onto lightly floured surface; gently roll in flour to coat. Knead lightly 10 times. Roll or pat ½ inch thick. Cut with floured 2½-inch biscuit cutter. Place about 1 inch apart on ungreased cookie sheet. Bake 10 to 12 minutes or until golden brown. Immediately remove from cookie sheet. Serve hot. *About 10 biscuits.*

Buttermilk-Rye Biscuits

Rye flour absorbs more liquid as it stands. So even if the dough seems a little dry, resist the temptation to add more buttermilk. Little sandwiches made with corned beef and honey mustard are especially good on these hearty biscuits.

> ½ cup shortening
> 1¼ cups all-purpose flour
> ¾ cup rye flour
> 2 teaspoons baking powder
> 2 teaspoons caraway seed
> 1 teaspoon salt
> ½ teaspoon baking soda
> About ¾ cup buttermilk

Heat oven to 450°. Cut shortening into flours, baking powder, caraway seed, salt and baking soda with pastry blender in large bowl until mixture resembles fine crumbs. Stir in just enough buttermilk so dough leaves side of bowl and forms a ball.

Turn dough onto lightly floured surface; gently roll in flour to coat. Knead lightly 10 times. Roll or pat ½ inch thick. Cut with floured 2½-inch biscuit cutter. Place about 1 inch apart on ungreased cookie sheet. Bake 10 to 12 minutes or until golden brown. Immediately remove from cookie sheet. Serve hot. *About 10 biscuits.*

Baking Powder Biscuits

¹/₂ cup shortening
2 cups all-purpose flour
1 tablespoon sugar
3 teaspoons baking powder
1 teaspoon salt
About ³/₄ cup milk

Heat oven to 450°. Cut shortening into flour, sugar, baking powder and salt with pastry blender in large bowl until mixture resembles fine crumbs. Stir in just enough milk so dough leaves side of bowl and forms a ball.

Turn dough onto lightly floured surface; gently roll in flour to coat. Knead lightly 10 times. Roll or pat ¹/₂ inch thick. Cut with floured 2¹/₂-inch biscuit cutter. Place about 1 inch apart on ungreased cookie sheet. Bake 10 to 12 minutes or until golden brown. Immediately remove from cookie sheet. Serve hot. *About 10 biscuits.*

Cornmeal Biscuits

You can use yellow, white or blue cornmeal in this recipe.

¹/₂ cup shortening
1¹/₂ cups all-purpose flour
¹/₂ cup cornmeal
1 tablespoon sugar
3 teaspoons baking powder
1 teaspoon salt
About ³/₄ cup milk
Cornmeal

Heat oven to 450°. Cut shortening into flour, ¹/₂ cup cornmeal, the sugar, baking powder and salt with pastry blender in large bowl until mixture resembles fine crumbs. Stir in just enough milk so dough leaves side of bowl and forms a ball.

Turn dough onto lightly floured surface; gently roll in flour to coat. Knead lightly 10 times. Roll or pat ¹/₂ inch thick. Cut with floured 2¹/₂-inch biscuit cutter. Place about 1 inch apart on ungreased cookie sheet. Sprinkle lightly with cornmeal. Bake 10 to 12 minutes or until golden brown. Immediately remove from cookie sheet. Serve hot. *About 10 biscuits.*

Making the Perfect Biscuit

Measuring

- Carefully measure dry ingredients into a large bowl. Accurate measurement helps to ensure best baking results.

Mixing

- Using a pastry blender with a rocking motion, or two knives in a crisscross cutting motion, cut the shortening into the dry ingredients until the mixture resembles fine crumbs. If the shortening isn't cut in enough, the biscuits won't be flaky. If the shortening is cut in too much, the biscuits will be crumbly.
- Use a fork to stir the milk into the flour mixture just until the dough leaves the side of the bowl and forms a ball. Overmixing will result in less tender biscuits. Too much milk makes dough sticky; not enough makes biscuits dry.

Kneading

- Place the dough on a lightly floured surface. Gently roll the dough to coat it with flour to prevent sticking.
- Knead the dough lightly ten times. To knead, fold the dough in half toward you. With the heels of your hands, press and push the dough away from you in a quick, short, rocking motion. Give the dough a quarter turn and repeat.
- If the dough sticks, sprinkle just enough additional flour onto the surface to prevent sticking.

Cut shortening into flour mixture until the mixture resembles fine crumbs.

Stir in enough milk until dough leaves side of bowl (dough will be soft).

Roll or pat the dough ¹/₂ inch thick. Cut with floured 2¹/₂-inch round cutter.

Rolling

- Roll the dough with a lightly floured rolling pin or pat the dough with lightly floured hands to ¹/₂-inch thickness. Use a ruler to measure.

Cutting

- Cut the dough using a biscuit cutter dipped into flour. Cut the biscuits out of the dough as close together as possible. Push the cutter straight into the dough. Twisting the cutter as you cut will result in uneven biscuits.
- After you've cut out as many biscuits as you can, press the scraps of dough together lightly, but do not knead. Roll or pat the remaining dough to ¹/₂-inch thickness and cut. The appearance of these biscuits will be slightly irregular, but the flavor and texture will be perfectly acceptable.
- If you don't have a biscuit cutter, pat dough into an 8-inch square, and cut into nine squares using a sharp knife.
- To make quick drop biscuits, add 1 or 2 tablespoons more of liquid to make a slightly soft dough. Do not turn dough onto lightly floured surface to knead. Instead, drop dough by rounded tablespoonfuls onto lightly greased cookie sheet. Bake as directed.

Baking

- Place oven rack in center position for the best circulation of heat.
- Place unbaked biscuits on an ungreased shiny cookie sheet. A dark, nonstick or dull cookie sheet can result in biscuits with dark brown bottoms. If you have a dark cookie sheet, reduce the oven temperature by 25°.
- For biscuits with soft sides, place biscuits with sides touching on an ungreased shiny pan.
- Bake until golden brown. Immediately remove from cookie sheet; serve hot.

Reheating

- To reheat biscuits in your microwave, place desired number of biscuits on a microwavable paper towel or napkin. Microwave uncovered on medium (50%) just until warm—one biscuit for 15 to 30 seconds, two for 25 to 40 seconds, three for 35 to 60 seconds and four biscuits for 45 seconds to 1 minute 15 seconds. Or to reheat in a conventional oven, wrap biscuits in aluminum foil and heat in 400° oven about 5 minutes or until warm.

Basil-Pepper Biscuits

¹/₂ cup shortening
2 cups all-purpose flour
2 tablespoons chopped fresh or 2 tea-
* spoons dried basil leaves*
3 teaspoons baking powder
1 teaspoon salt
1 teaspoon cracked black pepper
About ³/₄ cup milk

Heat oven to 450°. Cut shortening into flour, basil, baking powder, salt and pepper with pastry blender in large bowl until mixture resembles fine crumbs. Stir in just enough milk so dough leaves side of bowl and forms a ball.

Turn dough onto lightly floured surface; gently roll in flour to coat. Knead lightly 10 times. Roll or pat ¹/₂ inch thick. Cut with floured 2¹/₂-inch biscuit cutter. Place about 1 inch apart on ungreased cookie sheet. Bake 10 to 12 minutes or until golden brown. Immediately remove from cookie sheet. Serve hot. *About 10 biscuits.*

Pesto Biscuits

You can make your own pesto or buy it— either way, these biscuits will be delicious!

¹/₃ cup shortening
¹/₄ cup pesto
2 cups all-purpose flour
3 teaspoons baking powder
¹/₂ teaspoon salt
About ¹/₂ cup milk
Grated Parmesan cheese

Heat oven to 450°. Cut shortening and pesto into flour, baking powder and salt with pastry blender in large bowl until mixture resembles fine crumbs. Stir in just enough milk so dough leaves side of bowl and forms a ball.

Turn dough onto lightly floured surface; gently roll in flour to coat. Knead lightly 10 times. Roll or pat ¹/₂ inch thick. Cut with floured 2¹/₂-inch biscuit cutter. Place about 1 inch apart on ungreased cookie sheet. Sprinkle with cheese. Bake 10 to 12 minutes or until golden brown. Immediately remove from cookie sheet. Serve hot. *About 10 biscuits.*

Pesto Biscuits, Sour Cream–Chive Biscuit Sticks
(page 38)

Country-style Butter Biscuits

1/3 cup shortening
2 cups all-purpose flour
3 teaspoons baking powder
1 teaspoon salt
1/4 cup (1/2 stick) firm butter or margarine
About 3/4 cup milk

Heat oven to 450°. Cut shortening into flour, baking powder and salt with pastry blender in large bowl until mixture resembles fine crumbs. Cut butter into 1/4-inch pieces; toss with flour mixture. Stir in just enough milk so dough leaves side of bowl and forms a ball.

Turn dough onto lightly floured surface; gently roll in flour to coat. Knead lightly 10 times. Roll or pat 1/2 inch thick. Cut with floured 3-inch biscuit cutter. Place about 1 inch apart on ungreased cookie sheet. Bake 12 to 15 minutes or until golden brown. Immediately remove from cookie sheet. Brush with softened butter or margarine if desired. Serve hot. *About 8 biscuits.*

Angel Biscuits

Yeast helps to make these biscuits light. If you want even lighter biscuits, cover and let unbaked biscuits rise in a warm place for about 30 minutes or until puffy. Bake as directed.

1 package regular or quick-acting active dry yeast
2 tablespoons warm water (105° to 115°)
1/2 cup shortening
2 1/2 cups all-purpose flour
3 tablespoons sugar
1 1/2 teaspoons baking powder
1/2 teaspoon baking soda
1/2 teaspoon salt
About 1 cup buttermilk

Heat oven to 400°. Dissolve yeast in warm water; reserve. Cut shortening into flour, sugar, baking powder, baking soda and salt with pastry blender in large bowl until mixture resembles fine crumbs. Stir in yeast mixture and just enough buttermilk so dough leaves side of bowl and forms a ball.

Turn dough onto generously floured surface; gently roll in flour to coat. Knead lightly 25 to 30 times, sprinkling with flour if dough is too sticky. Roll or pat 1/2 inch thick. Cut with floured 2 1/2-inch biscuit cutter. Place about 1 inch apart on ungreased cookie sheet. Bake 12 to 14 minutes or until golden brown. Immediately remove from cookie sheet. Brush with softened margarine or butter if desired. Serve hot. *About 15 biscuits.*

Easy Cream Biscuits

These biscuits are even easier than most! Because cream is used, you don't have to worry about cutting shortening into the flour.

> *About 1¹/₄ cups whipping (heavy) cream*
> *1³/₄ cups all-purpose flour*
> *2¹/₂ teaspoons baking powder*
> *¹/₂ teaspoon salt*

Heat oven to 450°. Stir just enough whipping cream into remaining ingredients in large bowl so dough leaves side of bowl and forms a ball. (If dough is too dry, mix in 1 to 2 teaspoons additional whipping cream.)

Turn dough onto lightly floured surface; gently roll in flour to coat. Knead lightly 10 times, sprinkling with flour if dough is too sticky. Roll or pat ¹/₂ inch thick. Cut with floured 2-inch biscuit cutter. Place about 1 inch apart on ungreased cookie sheet. Bake 10 to 12 minutes or until golden brown. Immediately remove from cookie sheet. Serve hot. *About 12 biscuits.*

Breakfast Sausage Biscuits

Making a delicious breakfast sandwich is a snap with these biscuits. Use a 3-inch biscuit cutter and bake the biscuits just a few minutes longer. Split the warm biscuits and fill with eggs and cheese.

> *¹/₂ pound bulk pork sausage*
> *¹/₃ cup shortening*
> *2 cups all-purpose flour*
> *3 teaspoons baking powder*
> *¹/₄ teaspoon salt*
> *About ³/₄ cup milk*

Heat oven to 450°. Cook sausage in 10-inch skillet over medium heat, stirring frequently, until brown. Drain if necessary. Cool sausage slightly; crumble.

Cut shortening into flour, baking powder and salt with pastry blender in large bowl until mixture resembles fine crumbs. Stir in sausage. Stir in just enough milk so dough leaves side of bowl and forms a ball.

Turn dough onto lightly floured surface; gently roll in flour to coat. Knead lightly 10 times. Roll or pat ¹/₂ inch thick. Cut with floured 2¹/₂-inch biscuit cutter. Place about 1 inch apart on ungreased cookie sheet. Bake 10 to 12 minutes or until golden brown. Immediately remove from cookie sheet. Serve hot. Refrigerate any remaining biscuits. *About 10 biscuits.*

Toasted Sesame–Cheese Biscuits

To toast sesame seed, heat oven to 350° and bake in an ungreased pan 10 to 12 minutes, stirring occasionally, until golden brown. Or heat sesame seed in an ungreased skillet over medium heat about 2 minutes, stirring occasionally, until golden brown.

>   *¹/₃ cup shortening*
>   *2 cups all-purpose flour*
>   *3 teaspoons baking powder*
>   *¹/₂ teaspoon salt*
>   *¹/₂ cup shredded Cheddar or Colby cheese*
>   *¹/₄ cup sesame seed, toasted*
>   *About ³/₄ cup milk*
>   *Sesame seed*

Heat oven to 450°. Cut shortening into flour, baking powder and salt with pastry blender in large bowl until mixture resembles fine crumbs. Stir in cheese and ¹/₄ cup sesame seed. Stir in just enough milk so dough leaves side of bowl and forms a ball.

Turn dough onto lightly floured surface; gently roll in flour to coat. Knead lightly 10 times. Roll or pat ¹/₂ inch thick. Cut with floured 2¹/₂-inch biscuit cutter. Place about 1 inch apart on ungreased cookie sheet. Sprinkle lightly with sesame seed. Bake 10 to 12 minutes or until golden brown. Immediately remove from cookie sheet. Serve hot. *About 12 biscuits.*

Sour Cream–Chive Biscuit Sticks

You can make fun shapes by tying the dough strips into loose knots or twisting them into pretzel shapes.

>   *¹/₃ cup shortening*
>   *2 cups all-purpose flour*
>   *3 teaspoons baking powder*
>   *¹/₂ teaspoon salt*
>   *2 tablespoons chopped fresh or freeze-dried chives*
>   *1¹/₄ cups sour cream*
>   *2 tablespoons margarine or butter, melted*
>   *Poppy seed, sesame seed or coarse salt*

Heat oven to 450°. Cut shortening into flour, baking powder and salt with pastry blender in large bowl until mixture resembles fine crumbs. Stir in chives. Stir in sour cream until dough leaves side of bowl and forms a ball.

Turn dough onto lightly floured surface; gently roll in flour to coat. Knead lightly 10 times. Roll or pat into rectangle, 12 × 8 inches. Cut rectangle crosswise into 12 strips, 8 × 1 inch. Twist each strip. Place about 1 inch apart on ungreased cookie sheet. Brush strips lightly with margarine. Sprinkle with poppy seed. Bake 10 to 12 minutes or until golden brown. Immediately remove from cookie sheet. Serve hot. *12 biscuit sticks.*

Orange–Chocolate Chip Biscuits

¹/₃ cup shortening
2 cups all-purpose flour
2 tablespoons sugar
3 teaspoons baking powder
2 teaspoons grated orange peel
¹/₂ teaspoon salt
¹/₄ cup miniature semisweet chocolate chips
About ²/₃ cup orange juice
Orange Glaze (below)

Heat oven to 450°. Cut shortening into flour, sugar, baking powder, orange peel and salt with pastry blender in large bowl until mixture resembles fine crumbs. Stir in chocolate chips. Stir in just enough orange juice so dough leaves side of bowl and forms a ball.

Turn dough onto lightly floured surface; gently roll in flour to coat. Knead lightly 10 times. Roll or pat ¹/₂ inch thick. Cut with floured 2¹/₂-inch biscuit cutter. Place about 1 inch apart on ungreased cookie sheet. Bake 10 to 12 minutes or until golden brown. Immediately remove from cookie sheet. Brush Orange Glaze over warm biscuits. Serve warm. *About 10 biscuits.*

ORANGE GLAZE

¹/₄ cup powdered sugar
2 teaspoons orange juice

Mix ingredients until smooth.

Glazed Cinnamon-Raisin Biscuits

2¹/₂ cups Bisquick Original baking mix
¹/₂ cup raisins
¹/₂ teaspoon ground cinnamon
¹/₄ cup (¹/₂ stick) firm margarine or butter, cut into ¹/₄-inch pieces
About ²/₃ cup milk
Glaze (below)

Heat oven to 450°. Stir baking mix, raisins and cinnamon in large bowl until blended; toss with margarine. Add just enough milk so dough leaves side of bowl and forms a ball.

Turn dough onto surface generously dusted with baking mix; gently roll in baking mix to coat. Knead lightly 5 times. Roll or pat ¹/₂ inch thick. Cut with 3-inch biscuit cutter dipped into baking mix. Place about 1 inch apart on ungreased cookie sheet. Bake about 9 minutes or until golden brown. Immediately remove from cookie sheet. Spread Glaze over warm biscuits. Serve warm. *About 8 biscuits.*

GLAZE

1 cup powdered sugar
4 to 6 teaspoons water

Mix ingredients until smooth and spreading consistency.

Making the Perfect Popover

Preheating

- Popovers need steam to rise, so a very hot oven is required. The batter is quick to prepare, so make sure you turn your oven on first to allow enough time for it to reach the correct temperature. If your oven isn't hot enough, your popovers won't "pop."

Greasing

- Generously grease popover pan, medium muffin cups ($2\frac{1}{2} \times 1\frac{1}{4}$ inches) or 6-ounce custard cups. Popovers may stick if the cups aren't greased well.

Mixing

- Beat the eggs slightly in a medium bowl. Be sure the bowl you use is large enough so you can stir in the other ingredients easily.
- Beat in the remaining ingredients just until the mixture is smooth. Overbeating will result in popovers that don't rise fully.

Filling Cups

- Divide the batter evenly among cups. To ensure even baking, the popovers should all be the same size.
- The deeper the cups, the higher the popovers will be.

Baking

- Bake 20 minutes. Reduce oven temperature to 350°. Starting popovers in a 450° oven helps them rise. Reducing the oven temperature allows them to bake completely without burning.
- Immediately remove popovers from the cups, and serve hot. Allowing them to stand in the cups will result in soft instead of crisp sides.

Whole Wheat Popovers

2 eggs
¾ cup all-purpose flour
¼ cup whole wheat flour
1 cup milk
½ teaspoon salt

Heat oven to 450°. Generously grease 6-cup popover pan, six 6-ounce custard cups or 8 medium muffin cups, 2½ × 1¼ inches. Beat eggs slightly in medium bowl. Beat in flours, milk and salt just until smooth (do not overbeat).

Divide batter evenly among cups. Bake 20 minutes. Reduce oven temperature to 350°. Bake 20 minutes longer. Immediately remove from cups. Serve hot. *6 popovers.*

TRADITIONAL POPOVERS: Omit whole wheat flour; increase all-purpose flour to 1 cup.

Garlic-Basil Popovers

If you'd like a milder garlic flavor, use only 1 clove of garlic.

2 eggs
1 tablespoon chopped fresh or 1 teaspoon dried basil leaves
2 cloves garlic, finely chopped (about 1 teaspoon)
1 cup all-purpose flour
1 cup milk
½ teaspoon salt

Heat oven to 450°. Generously grease 6-cup popover pan, six 6-ounce custard cups or 8 medium muffin cups, 2½ × 1¼ inches. Beat eggs, basil and garlic slightly in medium bowl. Beat in flour, milk and salt just until smooth (do not overbeat).

Divide batter evenly among cups. Bake 20 minutes. Reduce oven temperature to 350°. Bake 20 minutes longer. Immediately remove from cups. Serve hot. *6 popovers.*

Cinnamon Biscuit Fans

¹/₃ cup firm margarine or butter
2 cups all-purpose flour
2 tablespoons sugar
3 teaspoons baking powder
¹/₂ teaspoon salt
About ³/₄ cup milk
3 tablespoons margarine or butter,
   softened
3 tablespoons sugar
1 teaspoon ground cinnamon
Glaze (below)

Heat oven to 425°. Grease 8 medium muffin cups, 2¹/₂ × 1¹/₄ inches. Cut ¹/₃ cup margarine into flour, 2 tablespoons sugar, the baking powder and salt with pastry blender in large bowl until mixture resembles fine crumbs. Stir in just enough milk so dough leaves side of bowl and forms a ball.

Turn dough onto lightly floured surface; gently roll in flour to coat. Knead lightly 10 times. Roll into rectangle, 12 × 10 inches. Spread 3 tablespoons margarine over rectangle. Mix 3 tablespoons sugar and the cinnamon; sprinkle over rectangle. Cut rectangle crosswise into 6 strips, 10 × 2 inches. Stack strips; cut crosswise into 8 pieces. Place cut sides up in muffin cups. Bake 16 to 18 minutes or until golden brown. Immediately remove from pan. Drizzle Glaze over warm biscuits. *8 biscuits.*

GLAZE

¹/₂ cup powdered sugar
2 to 2¹/₂ teaspoons milk

Mix ingredients until smooth and drizzling consistency.

Cinnamon Biscuit Fans, Breakfast Sausage Biscuits (page 37)

Raisin-Oat Scones

¹/₃ cup firm margarine or butter
1¹/₂ cups all-purpose flour
¹/₄ cup packed brown sugar
2¹/₂ teaspoons baking powder
¹/₂ teaspoon ground cinnamon
¹/₄ teaspoon salt
¹/₂ cup quick-cooking or regular oats
¹/₂ cup raisins
1 egg
About ¹/₂ cup whipping (heavy) cream

Heat oven to 400°. Cut margarine into flour, brown sugar, baking powder, cinnamon and salt with pastry blender in large bowl until mixture resembles fine crumbs. Stir in oats and raisins. Stir in egg and just enough whipping cream so dough leaves side of bowl and forms a ball.

Turn dough onto lightly floured surface; gently roll in flour to coat. Knead lightly 10 times. Pat or roll into 8-inch circle on ungreased cookie sheet. Cut into 8 wedges, but do not separate. Brush with whipping cream and sprinkle with oats if desired. Bake 16 to 18 minutes or until golden brown. Immediately remove from cookie sheet; carefully separate wedges. Serve warm. *8 scones.*

Apple-Date Scones

¹/₃ cup firm margarine or butter
1¹/₂ cups all-purpose flour
2 tablespoons sugar
2 teaspoons baking powder
¹/₂ teaspoon ground cinnamon
¹/₄ teaspoon salt
¹/₂ cup quick-cooking or regular oats
¹/₂ cup chopped unpeeled apple (about 1 small)
¹/₄ cup chopped dates
1 egg
About ¹/₃ cup half-and-half

Heat oven to 400°. Cut margarine into flour, sugar, baking powder, cinnamon and salt with pastry blender in large bowl until mixture resembles fine crumbs. Stir in oats, apple and dates. Stir in egg and just enough half-and-half so dough leaves side of bowl and forms a ball.

Turn dough onto lightly floured surface; gently roll in flour to coat. Knead lightly 10 times. Pat or roll into 8-inch circle on ungreased cookie sheet. Cut into 8 wedges, but do not separate. Brush with half-and-half and sprinkle with sugar if desired. Bake 16 to 18 minutes or until golden brown. Immediately remove from cookie sheet; carefully separate wedges. Serve warm. *8 scones.*

Maple-Nut Scones

2 tablespoons packed brown sugar
2 tablespoons finely chopped walnuts or almonds
¹/₂ cup (1 stick) firm margarine or butter
2 cups all-purpose flour
2 tablespoons packed brown sugar
2 teaspoons baking powder
¹/₄ teaspoon salt
¹/₂ cup coarsely chopped walnuts or almonds, toasted (see page 47)
¹/₃ cup pure maple syrup or maple-flavored syrup
1 egg
About 2 tablespoons milk
Milk

Heat oven to 400°. Mix 2 tablespoons brown sugar and 2 tablespoons finely chopped walnuts; reserve. Cut margarine into flour, 2 tablespoons brown sugar, the baking powder and salt with pastry blender in large bowl until mixture resembles fine crumbs. Stir in ¹/₂ cup walnuts. Stir in maple syrup, egg and just enough of the 2 tablespoons milk so dough leaves side of bowl and forms a ball.

Turn dough onto lightly floured surface; gently roll in flour to coat. Knead lightly 10 times. Pat or roll into 8-inch circle on ungreased cookie sheet. Brush with milk. Sprinkle with brown sugar–walnut mixture. Cut into 8 wedges, but do not separate. Bake 16 to 18 minutes or until golden brown. Immediately remove from cookie sheet; carefully separate wedges. Serve warm. *8 scones.*

Coconut-Pecan Scones

¹/₃ cup firm margarine or butter
1³/₄ cups all-purpose flour
3 tablespoons sugar
2 teaspoons baking powder
¹/₄ teaspoon salt
¹/₂ cup chopped pecans, toasted if desired (see page 47)
¹/₃ cup flaked coconut
1 egg
About ¹/₂ cup half-and-half
Half-and-half
Flaked coconut

Heat oven to 400°. Cut margarine into flour, sugar, baking powder and salt with pastry blender in large bowl until mixture resembles fine crumbs. Stir in pecans and ¹/₃ cup coconut. Stir in egg and just enough of the ¹/₂ cup half-and-half so dough leaves side of bowl and forms a ball.

Turn dough onto lightly floured surface; gently roll in flour to coat. Knead lightly 10 times. Pat or roll into 8-inch circle on ungreased cookie sheet. Cut into 8 wedges, but do not separate. Brush with half-and-half. Sprinkle with coconut. Bake 16 to 18 minutes or until golden brown. Immediately remove from cookie sheet; carefully separate wedges. Serve warm. *8 scones.*

Lemon–Cream Cheese Scones

¹/₃ cup firm margarine or butter
2¹/₄ cups all-purpose flour
¹/₄ cup sugar
1 tablespoon grated lemon peel
2 teaspoons baking powder
¹/₄ teaspoon salt
¹/₃ cup milk
1 package (3 ounces) cream cheese, softened
1 egg
Lemon juice
Sugar

Heat oven to 400°. Cut margarine into flour, ¹/₄ cup sugar, the lemon peel, baking powder and salt with pastry blender in large bowl until mixture resembles fine crumbs. Gradually stir milk into cream cheese in small bowl until smooth. Stir cream cheese mixture and egg into flour mixture until dough leaves side of bowl and forms a ball.

Turn dough onto lightly floured surface; gently roll in flour to coat. Knead lightly 10 times. Pat or roll into 9-inch circle on ungreased cookie sheet. Brush with lemon juice. Sprinkle with sugar. Cut into 8 wedges, but do not separate. Bake 16 to 18 minutes or until golden brown. Immediately remove from cookie sheet; carefully separate wedges. Serve warm. *8 scones.*

Almond-Crumb Scones

Crumb Topping (below)
¹/₂ cup (1 stick) firm margarine or butter
2 cups all-purpose flour
¹/₄ cup sugar
2¹/₂ teaspoons baking powder
¹/₄ teaspoon salt
¹/₂ cup chopped almonds, toasted†
1 egg
About ¹/₂ cup half-and-half

Heat oven to 400°. Prepare Crumb Topping; reserve. Cut margarine into flour, sugar, baking powder and salt with pastry blender in large bowl until mixture resembles fine crumbs. Stir in almonds. Stir in egg and just enough half-and-half so dough leaves side of bowl and forms a ball.

Turn dough onto lightly floured surface; gently roll in flour to coat. Knead lightly 10 times. Pat or roll into 9-inch circle on ungreased cookie sheet. Sprinkle with Crumb Topping; press lightly into dough. Cut into 8 wedges, but do not separate. Bake about 15 minutes or until golden brown. Immediately remove from cookie sheet; carefully separate wedges. Serve warm. *8 scones.*

CRUMB TOPPING

2 tablespoons firm margarine or butter
3 tablespoons all-purpose flour
2 tablespoons sugar
2 tablespoons finely chopped almonds,
    toasted†

Cut margarine into remaining ingredients until crumbly.

†To toast almonds and other nuts, heat oven to 350° and bake in an ungreased baking pan about 10 minutes, stirring occasionally, until golden brown.

Almond-Crumb Scones

Apricot–White Chocolate Scones

¹/₃ cup firm margarine or butter
1³/₄ cups all-purpose flour
¹/₄ cup sugar
2 teaspoons baking powder
¹/₄ teaspoon salt
¹/₃ cup finely chopped dried apricots
¹/₃ cup vanilla milk chips
1 egg
About ¹/₃ cup half-and-half

Heat oven to 400°. Cut margarine into flour, sugar, baking powder and salt with pastry blender in large bowl until mixture resembles fine crumbs. Stir in apricots and vanilla milk chips. Stir in egg and just enough half-and-half so dough leaves side of bowl and forms a ball.

Turn dough onto lightly floured surface; gently roll in flour to coat. Knead lightly 10 times. Pat or roll into 8-inch circle on ungreased cookie sheet. Cut into 8 wedges, but do not separate. Sprinkle with sugar if desired. Bake 16 to 18 minutes or until golden brown. Immediately remove from cookie sheet; carefully separate wedges. Serve warm. *8 scones.*

3
Oven-Fresh Coffee Cakes

A freshly baked coffee cake is reason enough to call up a group of friends and invite them over for a "coffee klatsch." Start baking these delicious coffee cakes, and you won't know when to stop! They're delicious and pretty, but only you will know the secret of how easy they are to prepare. Many recipes take less than an hour from start to finish—there's no long wait for dough to rise.

Morning and afternoon coffee breaks are a favorite American ritual. Wouldn't a homemade coffee cake make your gatherings even more special? From casual cakes such as Easy Pull-apart Coffee Cake to more formal, elegant cakes such as Danish Puff Coffee Cake and Sweet Potato–Caramel Twist Coffee Cake, there are recipes here for every occasion—whether it's an impromptu get-together at home, a morning meeting in the office, weekend brunch, an afternoon tea party or even enjoying some quiet time by yourself.

We love coffee cakes because they're sweet and rich. Fillings such as fruit, chocolate and nuts, and toppings such as caramel and streusel make these cakes ideal for anyone who craves luscious treats. While coffee cakes are terrific at breakfast or for dessert, they really are perfect for snacking. Perhaps that's the best thing about them—they're unabashedly luxurious. We don't *need* to have a midmorning snack, but it sure feels good when we do!

Cherry-Almond Coffee Cake (page 51)

Sour Cream–Apple Coffee Cake

Apple Filling (right)
1¹/₂ cups sugar
³/₄ cup (1¹/₂ sticks) margarine or butter, softened
1¹/₂ teaspoons vanilla
3 eggs
3 cups all-purpose flour
1¹/₂ teaspoons baking powder
1¹/₂ teaspoons baking soda
³/₄ teaspoon salt
1¹/₂ cups sour cream
Glaze (right)

Heat oven to 350°. Grease tube pan, 10 × 4 inches, or 12-cup bundt cake pan. Prepare Apple Filling; reserve. Beat sugar, margarine, vanilla and eggs in large bowl on medium speed 2 minutes, scraping bowl occasionally. Beat in flour, baking powder, baking soda and salt alternately with sour cream on low speed.

Spread ¹/₃ of the batter (about 2 cups) in pan. Sprinkle with ¹/₃ of the Apple Filling (about ¹/₃ cup). Repeat 2 times. Bake about 1 hour or until toothpick inserted near center comes out clean. Cool 20 minutes. Remove from pan; place on wire rack. Cool completely. Drizzle with Glaze. *16 servings.*

APPLE FILLING

1¹/₂ cups chopped peeled or unpeeled apples (about 1¹/₂ medium)
¹/₃ cup packed brown sugar
1 tablespoon all-purpose flour
2 tablespoons margarine or butter
¹/₄ teaspoon ground nutmeg
¹/₈ teaspoon salt
¹/₂ cup finely chopped nuts

Cook all ingredients except nuts in 1¹/₂-quart saucepan over medium heat 3 to 4 minutes, stirring constantly, until apples are tender. Stir in the nuts.

GLAZE

¹/₂ cup powdered sugar
¹/₄ teaspoon vanilla
1 to 2 teaspoons milk

Mix all ingredients until smooth and drizzling consistency.

Toasted Coconut–Banana Coffee Cake

2¹/₂ cups all-purpose flour
1¹/₄ cups sugar
1 cup coconut, toasted†
1 cup mashed ripe bananas
³/₄ cup (1¹/₂ sticks) margarine or butter, softened
¹/₂ cup plain yogurt
1¹/₄ teaspoons baking powder
1 teaspoon baking soda
1 teaspoon vanilla
¹/₄ teaspoon salt
2 eggs
Browned Butter Glaze (below)

Heat oven to 350°. Grease 12-cup bundt cake pan. Beat all ingredients except Browned Butter Glaze on low speed. Beat on medium speed 2 minutes, scraping bowl occasionally. Spread in pan. Bake 50 to 55 minutes or until toothpick inserted near center comes out clean. Cool 20 minutes. Remove from pan. Cool completely. Drizzle with glaze. *16 servings.*

BROWNED BUTTER GLAZE

2 tablespoons butter††
1¹/₂ cups powdered sugar
¹/₂ teaspoon vanilla
1 to 2 tablespoons milk

Heat butter over medium heat in 1¹/₂-quart saucepan until light brown. Stir in remaining ingredients until smooth and drizzling consistency. If too thick, stir in hot water, a few drops at a time, until desired consistency.

†To toast coconut, heat oven to 350° and bake coconut in an ungreased pan 5 to 7 minutes, stirring occasionally, until golden brown.

††We do not recommend margarine for this glaze.

Cherry-Almond Coffee Cake

If you use a tube pan with this recipe, you'll need to use about ¹/₂ cup finely chopped almonds to coat the pan.

¹/₃ cup finely chopped almonds
1 cup sugar
¹/₂ cup (1 stick) margarine or butter, softened
¹/₂ cup milk
¹/₂ teaspoon almond extract
1 container (15 ounces) ricotta cheese
2 eggs
2¹/₂ cups all-purpose flour
1 cup dried cherries or prunes, chopped
1 cup chopped almonds, toasted if desired (see page 47)
3 teaspoons baking powder
¹/₂ teaspoon salt

Heat oven to 350°. Grease 12-cup bundt cake pan or tube pan, 10 × 4 inches. Coat pan with ¹/₃ cup finely chopped almonds. Beat sugar, margarine, milk, almond extract, ricotta cheese and eggs in large bowl on low speed until blended. Beat on medium speed 2 minutes, scraping bowl occasionally. Beat in remaining ingredients (batter will be very thick). Spread in pan.

Bake 55 to 65 minutes or until toothpick inserted near center comes out clean. Cool 20 minutes. Remove from pan; place on wire rack. Sprinkle with powdered sugar if desired. Serve warm or let stand until cool. *16 servings.*

Easy Pull-apart Coffee Cake

1 cup pecan halves
³/₄ cup packed brown sugar
¹/₄ cup (¹/₂ stick) plus 2 tablespoons margarine or butter
2 tablespoons milk
1 package (6-serving size) vanilla regular pudding and pie filling
4 cups Bisquick Original baking mix
²/₃ cup milk
2 tablespoons granulated sugar
1 teaspoon vanilla
1 egg

Heat oven to 350°. Grease 12-cup bundt cake pan. Sprinkle pecan halves in pan. Heat brown sugar, margarine, 2 tablespoons milk and the pudding and pie filling (dry) in 1-quart saucepan over medium heat, stirring constantly, until mixture begins to boil around edge; remove from heat and reserve.

Mix remaining ingredients until stiff dough forms; beat 30 seconds. (If dough is too sticky, stir in additional baking mix.) Turn dough onto surface dusted with baking mix; roll in baking mix to coat. Knead lightly 10 times. Cut dough into 32 pieces. Stack pieces of dough in pan. Pour brown sugar mixture evenly over dough. Bake 25 to 30 minutes or until golden brown. Immediately invert onto heatproof serving plate; let pan remain over coffee cake 1 minute. Serve warm. *16 servings.*

Easy Pull-apart Coffee Cake, Fruit Swirl Coffee Cake (page 57)

Pineapple-Streusel Coffee Cake

Streusel Topping (below)
2¹/₂ cups all-purpose flour
1 cup sugar
¹/₂ cup (1 stick) margarine or butter, softened
¹/₂ cup pineapple yogurt
3 teaspoons baking powder
¹/₂ teaspoon salt
¹/₄ teaspoon baking soda
2 eggs
1 can (20 ounces) crushed pineapple in juice, well drained, and ²/₃ cup juice reserved

Heat oven to 350°. Prepare Streusel Topping; reserve. Mix flour, sugar, margarine, yogurt, baking powder, salt, baking soda, eggs and reserved pineapple juice. Spread in ungreased rectangular pan, 13 × 9 × 2 inches. Sprinkle with pineapple and Streusel Topping. Bake 45 to 50 minutes or until golden brown and toothpick inserted in center of cake (not pineapple) comes out clean. Serve warm or let stand until cool. *16 servings.*

STREUSEL TOPPING

¹/₂ cup (1 stick) firm margarine or butter
1 cup packed brown sugar
²/₃ cup all-purpose flour
1 teaspoon ground cinnamon
¹/₂ cup sliced almonds

Cut margarine into brown sugar, flour and cinnamon in medium bowl until crumbly. Stir in almonds.

Easy, Creative Coffee Cakes

Danish Puff Coffee Cake, with its crisp bottom crust and rich custard top, is perfect to serve at a special-occasion tea party or a casual family brunch. The helpful hints and how-to photos make this elegant coffee cake incredibly easy to make.

Danish Puff Coffee Cake

½ cup (1 stick) margarine or butter, softened
1 cup all-purpose flour
2 tablespoons cold water
½ cup (1 stick) margarine or butter
1 cup water
1 teaspoon almond extract
1 cup all-purpose flour
3 eggs
Glaze (right)
Chopped walnuts or pecans

Heat oven to 350°. Cut ½ cup margarine into 1 cup flour with pastry blender until particles are size of small peas. Sprinkle 2 tablespoons water over flour mixture; mix with fork. Gather pastry into ball; divide in half. Pat each half into rectangle, 12 × 3 inches, about 3 inches apart on ungreased cookie sheet.

Heat ½ cup margarine and 1 cup water to boiling in 2-quart saucepan; remove from heat. Quickly stir in almond extract and 1 cup flour. Stir vigorously over low heat about 1 minute or until mixture forms a ball; remove from heat. Add eggs; beat until smooth and glossy. Spread half of the topping evenly over each rectangle.

Bake about 1 hour or until topping is crisp and golden brown. Remove from cookie sheet; place on wire rack. Cool completely. Spread with Glaze. Sprinkle with walnuts. *12 servings.*

GLAZE

1½ cups powdered sugar
2 tablespoons margarine or butter, softened
1½ teaspoons vanilla
1 to 2 tablespoons warm water

Mix all ingredients until smooth and spreading consistency.

Pat each half of dough into rectangle, 12 × 3 inches, about 3 inches apart, on an ungreased cookie sheet.

Spread half of the egg mixture on each of the rectangles.

Helpful Hints:

- Use a pastry blender to cut margarine into flour until the particles are the size of small peas. If you don't have a pastry blender, use two knives in a crisscross cutting motion instead.
- Keep a ruler handy to measure as you pat the pastry into two 12 × 3-inch rectangles. Accurate measuring will help you make attractive coffee cakes.
- Measure the flour and have the almond extract and a measuring spoon at hand so you can add them to the boiling water mixture as soon as you remove it from the heat.
- After adding the eggs, be sure to beat the mixture until it's smooth and glossy. It might seem to take a while, but stick with it.
- As it bakes, the topping will puff up and then shrink and fall to form the custardy layer.
- Cooling the coffee cakes on wire racks helps to keep the bottom crusts crisp. Carefully slide the coffee cakes onto the wire racks, or lift each off of the cookie sheet using two pancake turners.
- Allow coffee cakes to cool completely before spreading with glaze. Glaze would soak into warm coffee cakes, making the top layers soggy.
- Slice coffee cakes with a long, thin-bladed knife using a light sawing motion.

Raspberry–Cream Cheese Coffee Cake

Even though this elegant coffee cake is made with yeast, it's quick because there's no kneading or long rising time.

1¹/₂ to 2 cups all-purpose flour
2 tablespoons sugar
2 tablespoons margarine or butter, softened
¹/₂ teaspoon salt
1 package regular or quick-acting active dry yeast
²/₃ cup very warm water (120° to 130°)
Cream Cheese Filling (right)
Streusel Topping (right)
1 jar (10 ounces) raspberry or strawberry preserves

Grease rectangular pan, 13 × 9 × 2 inches. Mix ³/₄ cup of the flour, the sugar, margarine, salt and yeast in large bowl. Stir in warm water. Beat on medium speed 2 minutes, scraping bowl occasionally. Stir in enough remaining flour until dough pulls away from side of bowl (dough will be sticky). Pat dough evenly in bottom and ¹/₂ inch up side of pan, using floured fingers. Cover and let rest 15 minutes.

Heat oven to 375°. Prepare Cream Cheese Filling and Streusel Topping; reserve. Bake crust 10 to 15 minutes or just until edges begin to brown. Spread Cream Cheese Filling over crust, almost to edges. Stir raspberry preserves; spoon evenly over filling. Sprinkle with Streusel Topping. Bake 20 to 25 minutes or just until almonds in topping begin to brown. Serve warm or let stand until cool. Refrigerate any remaining coffee cake. *12 servings.*

CREAM CHEESE FILLING

1 package (8 ounces) cream cheese, softened
¹/₄ cup sugar
¹/₂ teaspoon almond extract

Beat all ingredients on low speed about 1 minute or until smooth.

STREUSEL TOPPING

1 tablespoon firm margarine or butter
3 tablespoons all-purpose flour
3 tablespoons sugar
¹/₄ cup sliced almonds

Cut margarine into flour and sugar with pastry blender until crumbly. Stir in almonds.

Lemon Danish Coffee Cake

Make this cake your very own by substituting your favorite thick jam or preserves for some or all of the lemon curd. Lemon curd, a mixture of lemon juice, sugar, butter and egg yolks, can be found in gourmet shops, if it is not available in your grocery store.

³/₄ cup sugar
¹/₂ cup (1 stick) margarine or butter, softened
2 teaspoons grated lemon peel
³/₄ teaspoon baking powder
¹/₂ teaspoon vanilla
2 eggs
1¹/₂ cups all-purpose flour
1 jar (11¹/₄ ounces) lemon curd
Glaze (below)

Heat oven to 350°. Grease rectangular pan, 13 × 9 × 2 inches. Beat sugar, margarine, lemon peel, baking powder, vanilla and eggs in large bowl on low speed until blended. Beat on medium speed 2 minutes, scraping bowl occasionally (mixture will look curdled). Stir in flour. Spread in pan.

Spoon lemon curd by level tablespoonfuls about ³/₄ inch apart onto batter. Bake 23 to 26 minutes or until golden brown. Cool 15 minutes. Drizzle Glaze over warm coffee cake. Serve warm or let stand until cool. *15 servings.*

GLAZE

1 cup powdered sugar
5 to 6 teaspoons lemon juice

Mix ingredients until smooth and drizzling consistency.

Fruit Swirl Coffee Cake

For a smaller coffee cake, substitute 1 jar (10 ounces) any flavor fruit preserves for the pie filling and cut the remaining ingredients in half. Grease a 9 × 9 × 2-inch pan instead of the jelly roll pan, and prepare as directed.

1¹/₂ cups sugar
¹/₂ cup (1 stick) margarine or butter, softened
¹/₂ cup shortening
1¹/₂ teaspoons baking powder
1 teaspoon vanilla
1 teaspoon almond extract
4 eggs
3 cups all-purpose flour
1 can (21 ounces) cherry, apricot or blueberry pie filling
Glaze (below)

Heat oven to 350°. Generously grease jelly roll pan, 15¹/₂ × 10¹/₂ × 1 inch. Beat sugar, margarine, shortening, baking powder, vanilla, almond extract and eggs in large bowl on low speed, scraping bowl constantly. Beat on high speed 3 minutes, scraping bowl occasionally. Stir in flour. Spread ²/₃ of the batter in pan. Spread pie filling over batter. Drop remaining batter by tablespoonfuls onto pie filling. Bake about 45 minutes. Drizzle Glaze over warm coffee cake. Serve warm or let stand until cool. *18 servings.*

GLAZE

1 cup powdered sugar
1 to 2 tablespoons milk

Mix ingredients until smooth and drizzling consistency.

Orange Marmalade Coffee Cake

1/2 cup orange marmalade
1/4 cup sliced almonds
3 tablespoons margarine or butter, melted
2 tablespoons light corn syrup
2 1/4 cups all-purpose flour
1/4 cup sugar
1 tablespoon grated orange peel
3 teaspoons baking powder
1/2 teaspoon salt
About 1 cup half-and-half

Heat oven to 375°. Mix marmalade, almonds, margarine and corn syrup in round pan, 9 × 1 1/2 inches, or square pan, 8 × 8 × 2 inches. Mix flour, sugar, orange peel, baking powder and salt in medium bowl. Stir in just enough half-and-half so dough leaves side of bowl and forms a ball. Drop dough by 12 rounded tablespoonfuls onto marmalade mixture; flatten slightly.

Bake 30 to 35 minutes or until golden brown. Immediately invert onto heatproof serving plate; let pan remain over coffee cake 1 minute. Serve warm or let stand until cool. *8 servings.*

Blueberry Coffee Cake

Crumb Topping (below)
2 cups all-purpose flour
3/4 cup sugar
1/4 cup shortening
3/4 cup milk
2 1/2 teaspoons baking powder
3/4 teaspoon salt
2 cups fresh or frozen (thawed and drained) blueberries
Glaze (below)

Heat oven to 375°. Grease round pan, 9 × 1 1/2 inches, or square pan, 8 × 8 × 2 inches. Prepare Crumb Topping; reserve. Mix remaining ingredients except blueberries and Glaze; beat 30 seconds. Fold in blueberries. Spread in pan. Sprinkle with Crumb Topping. Bake 45 to 50 minutes or until toothpick inserted in center of cake (not blueberries) comes out clean. Cool 10 minutes. Remove from pan if desired. Drizzle Glaze over warm coffee cake. Serve warm or let stand until cool. *8 servings.*

CRUMB TOPPING

1/4 cup (1/2 stick) firm margarine or butter
1/2 cup sugar
1/3 cup all-purpose flour
1/2 teaspoon ground cinnamon

Cut margarine into remaining ingredients with pastry blender until crumbly.

GLAZE

1/2 cup powdered sugar
1/4 teaspoon vanilla
1 1/2 to 2 teaspoons hot water

Mix all ingredients until smooth and drizzling consistency.

Blueberry Coffee Cake, Blueberry-Oatmeal Bread (page 76)

Chocolate Swirl Coffee Cake

Topping (below)
2 cups Bisquick Original baking mix
1/4 cup sugar
2/3 cup water or milk
2 tablespoons margarine or butter,
   melted
1 egg
1/3 cup semisweet chocolate chips,
   melted

Heat oven to 400°. Grease square pan, 8 × 8 × 2 inches. Prepare Topping; reserve. Mix baking mix, sugar, water, margarine and egg; beat vigorously 30 seconds. Spread in pan. Spoon chocolate over batter; cut through batter and chocolate with knife several times to marble. Sprinkle with Topping. Bake 20 to 25 minutes or until brown and cake feels firm when touched in center. Serve warm or let stand until cool. *9 servings.*

TOPPING

1/3 cup flaked coconut
1/4 cup sugar
1/4 cup chopped walnuts or pecans
1 tablespoon margarine or butter,
   melted

Mix all ingredients.

Chocolate Chip–Fresh Mint Coffee Cake

For an extra-minty coffee cake, use mint chocolate chips in the batter and Topping.

Topping (below)
2 cups all-purpose flour
1 cup sugar
1/2 cup (1 stick) margarine or butter,
   softened
1 cup milk
1 tablespoon chopped fresh or 1 tea-
   spoon dried mint leaves
2 1/2 teaspoons baking powder
1/2 teaspoon salt
1 egg
1/2 cup semisweet chocolate chips

Heat oven to 350°. Grease square pan, 9 × 9 × 2 inches. Prepare Topping; reserve. Beat remaining ingredients except chocolate chips in large bowl on low speed 30 seconds. Beat on medium speed 2 minutes, scraping bowl occasionally. Stir in chocolate chips. Spread in pan. Sprinkle with Topping. Bake 40 to 45 minutes or until toothpick inserted in center comes out clean. Serve warm or let stand until cool. *9 servings.*

TOPPING

2 tablespoons firm margarine or butter
1/4 cup all-purpose flour
2 tablespoons sugar
1/4 cup semisweet chocolate chips

Cut margarine into flour and sugar with pastry blender until crumbly. Stir in chocolate chips.

Poppy Seed–Walnut Coffee Cake

Poppy Seed Filling (below)
2 cups all-purpose flour
3/4 cup packed brown sugar
1/3 cup margarine or butter, softened
1 cup milk
2 1/2 teaspoons baking powder
1/2 teaspoon salt
1/2 teaspoon ground cinnamon
1/4 teaspoon ground nutmeg
1 egg
1/2 cup chopped walnuts
1/4 cup chopped walnuts

Heat oven to 350°. Grease square pan, 9 × 9 × 2 inches. Prepare Poppy Seed Filling; reserve. Beat remaining ingredients except walnuts in large bowl on low speed until blended. Beat on medium speed 1 minute, scraping bowl occasionally. Stir in 1/2 cup walnuts. Spread half of the batter in pan. Spoon Poppy Seed Filling by small spoonfuls onto batter; carefully spread over batter. Spoon remaining batter over Poppy Seed Filling; carefully spread to cover Poppy Seed Filling. Sprinkle with 1/4 cup walnuts. Bake 40 to 45 minutes or until toothpick inserted in center comes out clean. Serve warm or let stand until cool. Sprinkle with powdered sugar if desired. *9 servings*.

POPPY SEED FILLING

1/3 cup poppy seed
1/3 cup walnuts
1/4 cup milk
1/4 cup honey

Place all ingredients in blender or food processor. Cover and blend on medium speed, stopping blender frequently to scrape sides, or process, until milk is absorbed.

Coconut-Caramel Coffee Cake

1/2 cup flaked coconut
3 tablespoons margarine or butter, melted
1 tablespoon water
1/3 cup packed brown sugar
3/4 cup chopped pecans
1 3/4 cups all-purpose flour
3/4 cup granulated sugar
1/4 cup shortening
1/2 cup milk
2 teaspoons baking powder
1/4 teaspoon salt
2 eggs
Apricot Cream Sauce (below)

Heat oven to 375°. Generously grease square pan, 8 × 8 × 2 inches. Press coconut in bottom of pan. Mix margarine, water, brown sugar and pecans; carefully spread over coconut. Mix remaining ingredients except Apricot Cream Sauce; beat vigorously 30 seconds. Spread batter in pan.

Bake 30 to 35 minutes or until toothpick inserted in center comes out clean. Immediately invert onto heatproof serving plate; let pan remain over coffee cake a few minutes. Serve warm or let stand until cool. Serve with Apricot Cream Sauce. *9 servings*.

APRICOT CREAM SAUCE

1/2 cup apricot preserves
1 cup sour cream or plain yogurt

Mix ingredients until well blended. Cover and refrigerate until serving time.

Raisin-Spice Coffee Cake

Streusel (below)
2 cups all-purpose flour
1 cup sugar
1/3 cup margarine or butter, softened
1 cup milk
3 teaspoons baking powder
1 teaspoon ground cinnamon
1/2 teaspoon salt
1/4 teaspoon ground nutmeg
1/4 teaspoon ground allspice
1 egg
1/2 cup raisins

Heat oven to 350°. Grease square pan, 9 × 9 × 2 inches. Prepare Streusel; reserve. Beat remaining ingredients except raisins in large bowl on low speed 30 seconds. Beat on medium speed 2 minutes, scraping bowl occasionally. Stir in raisins. Spread half of the batter in pan; sprinkle with half of the Streusel. Top with remaining batter; sprinkle with remaining Streusel. Bake 40 to 45 minutes or until toothpick inserted in center comes out clean. Serve warm or let stand until cool. *9 servings.*

STREUSEL

1/3 cup firm margarine or butter
1/2 cup all-purpose flour
1/3 cup packed brown sugar
1/2 teaspoon ground cinnamon
1/2 cup chopped walnuts or pecans

Cut margarine into flour, brown sugar and cinnamon with pastry blender until crumbly. Stir in walnuts.

Oatmeal-Plum Coffee Cake

If plums aren't available (or if you just really love pears) substitute 1½ cups chopped fresh pears for the plums. The results are equally delicious!

Streusel Topping (below)
1¾ cups all-purpose flour
1 cup packed brown sugar
3/4 cup quick-cooking or regular oats
1/2 cup (1 stick) margarine or butter, softened
1 cup buttermilk
3 teaspoons baking powder
1 teaspoon ground cinnamon
1/2 teaspoon baking soda
1/4 teaspoon salt
1/4 teaspoon ground nutmeg
1 egg
1½ cups chopped fresh plums

Heat oven to 350°. Grease square pan, 9 × 9 × 2 inches. Prepare Streusel Topping; reserve. Beat remaining ingredients except plums in large bowl on low speed 30 seconds. Beat on medium speed 2 minutes, scraping bowl occasionally. Stir in plums. Spread in pan. Sprinkle with Streusel Topping. Bake 50 to 55 minutes or until golden brown and toothpick inserted in center comes out clean. Serve warm or let stand until cool. *9 servings.*

STREUSEL TOPPING

2 tablespoons firm margarine or butter
1/4 cup all-purpose flour
2 tablespoons packed brown sugar
1/2 teaspoon ground cinnamon
1/4 cup quick-cooking or regular oats

Cut margarine into flour, brown sugar and cinnamon until crumbly. Stir in oats.

Sweet Potato–Caramel Twist Coffee Cake

If you buy canned sweet potatoes for this recipe, be sure to choose vacuum-packed sweet potatoes instead of those packed in syrup.

1/3 cup margarine or butter
1/2 cup packed brown sugar
1/4 cup corn syrup
1/2 cup chopped pecans
1/2 cup shortening
2 1/4 cups all-purpose flour
1/4 cup packed brown sugar
2 1/2 teaspoons baking powder
1/2 teaspoon salt
3/4 cup mashed cooked fresh or vacuum-
packed sweet potatoes
1/2 cup milk
2 tablespoons margarine or butter,
softened
3 tablespoons packed brown sugar

Heat oven to 400°. Heat 1/3 cup margarine in ungreased square pan, 9 × 9 × 2 inches, in oven until melted. Stir in 1/2 cup brown sugar and the corn syrup. Sprinkle with pecans.

Cut shortening into flour, 1/4 cup brown sugar, the baking powder and salt with pastry blender in large bowl until mixture resembles fine crumbs. Mix sweet potatoes and milk; stir into flour mixture until dough leaves side of bowl and forms a ball. Turn dough onto lightly floured surface; gently roll in flour to coat. Knead lightly 10 times.

Pat dough into 12-inch square. Spread 2 tablespoons margarine over dough. Sprinkle 3 tablespoons brown sugar over margarine. Fold dough into thirds; press edges together to seal. Cut crosswise into 1-inch strips. Twist ends of each strip in opposite directions. Arrange twists on pecans in pan. Bake 30 to 35 minutes or until golden brown. Immediately invert onto heatproof serving plate; let pan remain over coffee cake 1 minute. Serve warm. *9 servings.*

—————— ■ ——————

Papaya-Custard Coffee Cake

You'll know that a papaya is ripe if it yields slightly when you press on it.

1 cup all-purpose flour
1/2 cup milk
2 tablespoons granulated sugar
3 tablespoons margarine or butter,
melted
1 teaspoon baking powder
1/4 teaspoon salt
1 medium papaya, peeled and thinly
sliced
1 tablespoon lemon juice
1/4 cup granulated sugar
2/3 cup sour cream
1/2 teaspoon ground ginger
1 egg
Powdered sugar

Heat oven to 375°. Grease square pan, 9 × 9 × 2 inches. Mix flour, milk, 2 tablespoons granulated sugar, the margarine, baking powder and salt. Spread in pan. Toss papaya and lemon juice. Arrange papaya on batter in pan. Mix remaining ingredients except powdered sugar; pour over papaya.

Bake 25 to 30 minutes or until edges begin to pull away from sides of pan and center is set. Cool completely. Sprinkle with powdered sugar. Refrigerate any remaining coffee cake. *9 servings.*

Easy Creative Coffee Cakes

Braided Cream Cheese Coffee Cake is perfect when you need something that's quick to fix and delicious. Because you start with Bisquick Original baking mix, this pretty coffee cake with its tender, flaky crust and sweet cream cheese filling is surprisingly easy to make.

Braided Cream Cheese Coffee Cake

1 package (8 ounces) cream cheese, softened
1/3 cup sugar
1/4 teaspoon almond extract
1 package (3 ounces) cream cheese
1/4 cup (1/2 stick) firm margarine or butter
2 1/2 cups Bisquick Original baking mix
1/2 cup milk
Glaze (right)

Heat oven to 400°. Grease large cookie sheet. Mix 8-ounce package cream cheese, the sugar and almond extract until smooth; reserve. Cut 3-ounce package cream cheese and the margarine into baking mix in large bowl with pastry blender until particles are size of small peas. Stir in milk. Turn dough onto surface well dusted with baking mix; gently roll in baking mix to coat. Knead lightly 10 times. Roll into rectangle, 15 × 9 inches. Carefully place on cookie sheet.

Spread reserved cream cheese mixture in 4-inch strip lengthwise down center of rectangle. Make cuts 2 1/2 inches long at 1 inch intervals on each 15-inch side of rectangle. Fold strips over filling, overlapping and crossing in center. Bake about 20 minutes or until golden brown. Remove from cookie sheet; place on wire rack. Drizzle Glaze over warm coffee cake. Serve warm or let stand until cool. Refrigerate any remaining coffee cake. *12 servings.*

GLAZE

3/4 cup powdered sugar
1 tablespoon warm water
1/4 teaspoon almond extract

Mix all ingredients until smooth.

Fold strips of dough over filling, overlapping and crossing in center.

Helpful Hints:

- Because the dough will be rolled into a 15 × 9-inch rectangle, you'll need a cookie sheet at least 15 inches long and 9 inches wide.
- You can soften the cream cheese for the filling in your microwave. Remove the foil wrapper, and microwave the cream cheese uncovered on medium (50%) for 1 minute to 1 minute 30 seconds or until softened.
- Cut the margarine and cream cheese into the baking mix using a pastry blender or two knives in a crisscross cutting motion.
- You can knead the dough right on your countertop. If the dough sticks to it or your hands as you knead, sprinkle the countertop with a little more baking mix. To avoid a dry crust, add only enough baking mix to eliminate sticking.
- For the most attractive results, use a ruler to measure the dimensions of the dough as you shape it, the width of the cream cheese mixture as you spread it and the length and space between the cuts as you make them.
- Gently fold the dough rectangle in half or thirds and carefully lift and place on the cookie sheet. Unfold the dough. You might need to reshape it a little after unfolding.
- Carefully transfer the baked coffee cake to a wire rack to cool. It will cool faster on a wire rack, and the bottom crust won't become soggy from evaporating moisture that would be trapped between the crust and cookie sheet.
- You can decorate the top of the coffee cake to fit the occasion. Tint the Glaze pink for Valentine's Day, or decorate with cut-up candied cherries for Christmas.

Raspberry-Peach Coffee Cake

2 cups all-purpose flour
¹/₄ cup sugar
²/₃ cup milk
¹/₃ cup vegetable oil
2 teaspoons baking powder
¹/₂ teaspoon salt
1 cup cut-up dried peaches
¹/₂ cup red raspberry spreadable fruit or preserves
Powdered sugar or Glaze (below)

Heat oven to 350°. Grease cookie sheet. Mix flour, sugar, milk, oil, baking powder and salt with fork until dough leaves side of bowl and forms a ball. Turn dough onto lightly floured surface; gently roll in flour to coat. Knead lightly 10 times. Roll into 12-inch circle. (Turn dough over and sprinkle surface with more flour if necessary to prevent sticking.) Fold circle into fourths. Carefully place on cookie sheet and unfold.

Mix peaches and spreadable fruit. Spread over dough to within 3 inches of edge, mounding fruit in center. Bring dough up and over fruit, leaving about 3-inch opening in the center. Bake 30 to 35 minutes or until golden brown. Remove from cookie sheet; place on wire rack. Sprinkle with powdered sugar or drizzle Glaze over warm coffee cake. Serve warm or let stand until cool. *8 servings.*

GLAZE

¹/₂ cup powdered sugar
1 teaspoon light corn syrup
2 to 3 teaspoons hot water

Mix all ingredients until smooth and drizzling consistency.

Raspberry-Peach Coffee Cake, Braided Cream Cheese Coffee Cake (page 64)

Apple-filled Coffee Cake

¹/₄ cup shortening
2 cups all-purpose flour
2 tablespoons sugar
3 teaspoons baking powder
¹/₂ teaspoon salt
³/₄ milk
¹/₂ cup finely chopped peeled or unpeeled apple (about 1 small)
1 tablespoon sugar
¹/₂ teaspoon ground cinnamon
1 tablespoon margarine, melted
Glaze (below), if desired

Heat oven to 425°. Grease round pan, 8 × 1¹/₂ inches, or square pan, 8 × 8 × 2 inches. Cut shortening into flour, 2 tablespoons sugar, the baking powder and salt with pastry blender in large bowl until mixture resembles fine crumbs. Stir in milk until dough leaves side of bowl and forms a ball. Turn dough onto lightly floured surface; gently roll in flour to coat. Knead lightly 20 to 25 times. Divide dough into 12 equal parts; cover.

Mix apple, 1 tablespoon sugar and the cinnamon. Pat each part dough into 3-inch circle on floured surface. Place 1 rounded teaspoonful apple mixture in center of each circle. Bring edges of dough up over apple mixture; pinch and seal well to form a ball. Arrange balls, seam sides down, in pan. Brush with margarine. Bake 17 to 19 minutes or until golden brown. Drizzle Glaze over warm coffee cake. Serve warm or let stand until cool. *6 servings.*

GLAZE

¹/₃ cup powdered sugar
1¹/₂ teaspoons milk
¹/₈ teaspoon vanilla

Mix all ingredients until smooth.

4

Best-Loved Loaves and More

Traditional fruit- and nut-studded Cranberry Bread is a must for Thanksgiving. Zucchini Bread is wonderful during the harvest months. And Banana-Nut Bread is a favorite all year round. Quick-bread loaves are popular because they're so easy to make, they keep well in the refrigerator and, best of all, they're delicious!

Many of these breads are even better if you wait a day to slice them. Blueberry-Oatmeal Bread, therefore, might be the perfect addition to your breakfast—and you can make it the day before. Because they keep well, loaves make great gifts. Just wrap one up in plastic wrap and colored ribbons and include a jar of one of the jams on page 84; homemade bread is one of the most thoughtful gifts you can give.

We've included recipes here that will surprise and delight you. Of course there's classic Pumpkin Bread and Irish Soda Bread, but there are also new recipes for you to try. There's Pizza Loaf for pizza lovers, Bread Bowls to fill with chili or stew, and Cheesy Breadsticks for a party. You can play with recipes to make them into fun, different shapes. Our special feature on page 78 will show you how to transform your favorite loaf recipe into adorable mini loaves or unusual shapes. A homemade bread isn't just a great gift for someone else—bake a present for yourself, too!

Cranberry Bread (page 73)

Nut Bread

2 cups all-purpose flour
1 cup chopped walnuts or pecans,
   toasted if desired (see page 47)
1/2 cup whole wheat flour
1/2 cup granulated sugar
1/2 cup packed brown sugar
1 1/4 cups milk
1/3 cup vegetable oil
3 teaspoons baking powder
1/2 teaspoon salt
2 eggs

Heat oven to 350°. Grease bottoms only of 2 loaf pans, 8 1/2 × 4 1/2 × 2 1/2 inches, or 1 loaf pan, 9 × 5 × 3 inches. Mix all ingredients; beat 30 seconds. Pour into pans.

Bake 8-inch loaves 55 to 60 minutes, 9-inch loaf 60 to 65 minutes or until toothpick inserted in center comes out clean. Cool 5 minutes. Loosen sides of loaves from pans; remove from pans. Cool completely on wire rack before slicing. Store tightly wrapped in refrigerator up to 1 week. *2 loaves (12 slices each) or 1 loaf (24 slices).*

Banana-Nut Bread

1 1/4 cups sugar
1/2 cup (1 stick) margarine or butter,
   softened
2 eggs
1 1/2 cups mashed ripe bananas (about 3
   medium)
1/2 cup buttermilk
1 teaspoon vanilla
2 1/2 cups all-purpose flour
2 teaspoons baking powder
1/2 teaspoon salt
1/4 teaspoon baking soda
1 cup chopped walnuts or pecans

Heat oven to 350°. Grease bottoms only of 2 loaf pans, 8 1/2 × 4 1/2 × 2 1/2 inches, or 1 loaf pan, 9 × 5 × 3 inches. Mix sugar and margarine in large bowl. Stir in eggs. Add bananas, buttermilk and vanilla until smooth; beat until smooth. Stir in flour, baking powder, salt and baking soda just until flour is moistened. Stir in walnuts. Pour into pans.

Bake 8-inch loaves about 1 hour, 9-inch loaf about 1 hour 15 minutes or until toothpick inserted in center comes out clean. Cool 5 minutes. Loosen sides of loaves from pans; remove from pans. Cool completely on wire rack before slicing. Store tightly wrapped in refrigerator up to 1 week. *2 loaves (12 slices each) or 1 loaf (24 slices).*

Pumpkin Bread

1 cup sugar
1 cup canned pumpkin
1/3 cup vegetable oil
1 teaspoon vanilla
2 eggs
1 1/2 cups all-purpose flour
1/2 cup coarsely chopped walnuts or
  pecans
2 teaspoons baking powder
1/2 teaspoon ground cinnamon
1/4 teaspoon salt
1/4 teaspoon ground cloves

Heat oven to 350°. Grease bottom only of loaf pan, 8 1/2 × 4 1/2 × 2 1/2 or 9 × 5 × 3 inches. Mix sugar, pumpkin, oil, vanilla and eggs in large bowl. Stir in remaining ingredients. Pour into pan.

Bake 50 to 60 minutes or until toothpick inserted in center comes out clean. Cool 10 minutes. Loosen sides of loaf from pan; remove from pan. Cool completely on wire rack before slicing. Store tightly wrapped in refrigerator up to 1 week. *1 loaf (24 slices).*

Carrot-Nut Bread

1 1/2 cups shredded carrots (about 3
  medium)
3/4 cup sugar
1/3 cup vegetable oil
2 eggs
3/4 cup all-purpose flour
3/4 cup whole wheat flour
1/4 cup coarsely chopped walnuts or
  pecans
2 teaspoons baking powder
1/2 teaspoon salt
1/2 teaspoon ground cinnamon
1/2 teaspoon ground cloves

Heat oven to 350°. Grease bottom only of loaf pan, 8 1/2 × 4 1/2 × 2 1/2 or 9 × 5 × 3 inches. Mix carrots, sugar, oil and eggs in large bowl. Stir in remaining ingredients. Pour into pan.

Bake 50 to 60 minutes or until toothpick inserted in center comes out clean. Cool 10 minutes. Loosen sides of loaf from pan; remove from pan. Cool completely on wire rack before slicing. Store tightly wrapped in refrigerator up to 1 week. *1 loaf (24 slices).*

Making the Perfect Loaf

Greasing

- Grease the bottoms only of loaf pans. The batter will cling to the ungreased sides of the pan as it rises during baking and will form a nicely rounded top.
- Shiny metal pans give the best baking results. Even if you use dark, nonstick loaf pans, grease the bottoms as directed. Dark pans absorb heat more readily, so you'll minimize overbrowning by reducing the oven temperature by 25°.
- Use loaf pans that are the size specified in the recipe. If the recipe calls for two pans and you only have one, consider baking half of the batter in mini loaf pans, muffin cups or small cake molds (see Marvelous Mini Loaves, page 78).

Measuring

- Measure carefully to ensure best baking results.
- Chop or shred fruits, vegetables or nuts before you start making the batter. If you prepare the batter and then stop to chop or shred ingredients, the batter may become too stiff.

Mixing

- Mix the batter as directed in the recipe. To avoid overmixing, mix by hand instead of using an electric mixer.

Baking

- Position the oven rack in the center of the oven unless a recipe directs otherwise.
- Bake for the minimum time specified in the recipe, then check for doneness by inserting a long wooden toothpick or skewer into the center of the loaf. The toothpick may be moist from fruit or chocolate chips in the loaf, but it should not have wet batter clinging to it. If the loaf isn't done, bake a few minutes longer and test again.
- A large, lengthwise crack in the thin, tender top crust is to be expected.

Cooling

- Let loaves cool for about ten minutes in the pans, then loosen sides of loaves from pans and remove. Place loaves upright on a wire rack to cool.
- Allow loaves to cool completely before slicing. Some slice more easily after being stored in the refrigerator (wrapped) for a day.

Serving

- Slice the loaves using a sharp, thin-bladed knife in a light, sawing motion.
- After cooling, loaves can be wrapped tightly and refrigerated for a week.

Cranberry Bread

Fresh cranberries are available only during the fall and early winter. Why not buy a few extra bags to keep in your freezer? You can freeze them for up to a year.

2 cups fresh or frozen cranberries, chopped
1²/₃ cups sugar
²/₃ cup vegetable oil
¹/₂ cup milk
2 teaspoons grated lemon or orange peel
2 teaspoons vanilla
4 eggs
3 cups all-purpose flour
¹/₂ cup coarsely chopped walnuts or pecans
4 teaspoons baking powder
1 teaspoon salt

Heat oven to 350°. Grease bottoms only of 2 loaf pans, 8¹/₂ × 4¹/₂ × 2¹/₂ or 9 × 5 × 3 inches. Mix cranberries, sugar, oil, milk, lemon peel, vanilla and eggs in large bowl. Stir in remaining ingredients. Pour into pans.

Bake 50 to 60 minutes or until toothpick inserted in center comes out clean. Cool 10 minutes. Loosen sides of loaves from pans; remove from pans. Cool completely on wire rack before slicing. Store tightly wrapped in refrigerator up to 1 week. *2 loaves (24 slices each).*

Apple-Rhubarb Bread

1¹/₂ cups finely chopped rhubarb (about ¹/₂ pound)
1¹/₂ cups chopped peeled or unpeeled apples (about 1¹/₂ medium)
1¹/₂ cups sugar
¹/₂ cup vegetable oil
1 teaspoon vanilla
4 eggs
3 cups all-purpose flour
1 cup chopped walnuts or pecans, if desired
3¹/₂ teaspoons baking powder
1 teaspoon salt
1 teaspoon ground cinnamon

Heat oven to 350°. Grease bottoms only of 2 loaf pans, 8¹/₂ × 4¹/₂ × 2¹/₂ or 9 × 5 × 3 inches. Mix rhubarb, apples, sugar, oil, vanilla and eggs in large bowl. Stir in remaining ingredients. Pour into pans.

Bake 50 to 60 minutes or until toothpick inserted in center comes out clean. Cool 10 minutes. Loosen sides of loaves from pans; remove from pans. Cool completely on wire rack before slicing. Store tightly wrapped in refrigerator up to 1 week. *2 loaves (24 slices each).*

Zucchini Bread

Cut sliced Zucchini Bread into interesting shapes with cookie cutters. Spread the cut-outs with cream cheese for pretty (and delicious) treats.

3 cups shredded zucchini (about 3 medium)
1²/₃ cups sugar
²/₃ cup vegetable oil
2 teaspoons vanilla
4 eggs
3 cups all-purpose flour
¹/₂ cup coarsely chopped walnuts or pecans
¹/₂ cup raisins, if desired
4 teaspoons baking powder
1 teaspoon salt
1 teaspoon ground cinnamon
¹/₂ teaspoon ground cloves

Heat oven to 350°. Grease bottoms only of 2 loaf pans, 8½ × 4½ × 2½ or 9 × 5 × 3 inches. Mix zucchini, sugar, oil, vanilla and eggs in large bowl. Stir in remaining ingredients. Pour into pans.

Bake 50 to 60 minutes or until toothpick inserted in center comes out clean. Cool 10 minutes. Loosen sides of loaves from pans; remove from pans. Cool completely on wire rack before slicing. Store tightly wrapped in refrigerator up to 1 week. *2 loaves (24 slices each).*

Zucchini Bread, Banana-Nut Bread (page 70), Pumpkin Bread (page 71)

Oatmeal-Pineapple Bread

For a terrific toasted flavor, toast the oats and pecans according to the directions for toasting oats and walnuts on page 8.

³/₄ cup sugar
¹/₃ cup margarine or butter, melted
2 eggs
1 can (8 ounces) crushed pineapple, undrained
1³/₄ cups all-purpose flour
¹/₂ cup golden raisins
2¹/₂ teaspoons baking powder
1 teaspoon vanilla
¹/₂ teaspoon salt
¹/₄ teaspoon baking soda
1 cup quick-cooking or regular oats
¹/₂ cup chopped pecans

Heat oven to 350°. Grease bottom only of loaf pan, 8½ × 4½ × 2½ or 9 × 5 × 3 inches. Mix sugar, margarine, eggs and pineapple in large bowl. Stir in remaining ingredients except oats and pecans. Stir in oats and pecans. Pour into pan.

Bake 55 to 60 minutes or until toothpick inserted in center comes out clean. Cool 10 minutes. Loosen sides of loaf from pan; remove from pan. Cool completely on wire rack before slicing. Store tightly wrapped in refrigerator up to 1 week. *1 loaf (24 slices).*

Blueberry-Oatmeal Bread

²/₃ cup packed brown sugar
³/₄ cup milk
¹/₂ cup vegetable oil
2 eggs
2¹/₄ cups all-purpose flour
1 cup quick-cooking or regular oats
3 teaspoons baking powder
1 teaspoon ground cinnamon
¹/₄ teaspoon salt
1 cup fresh or frozen (thawed and drained) blueberries

Heat oven to 350°. Grease bottom only of loaf pan, 8¹/₂ × 4¹/₂ × 2¹/₂ or 9 × 5 × 3 inches. Mix brown sugar, milk, oil and eggs in large bowl. Stir in remaining ingredients except blueberries; beat 30 seconds. Fold in blueberries. Pour into pan. Sprinkle with oats if desired.

Bake 45 to 55 minutes or until toothpick inserted in center comes out clean. Cool 10 minutes. Loosen sides of loaf from pan; remove from pan. Cool completely on wire rack before slicing. Store tightly wrapped in refrigerator up to 1 week. *1 loaf (24 slices).*

Ginger-Pear Bread

3 cups chopped unpeeled pears (about 3 medium)
1¹/₄ cups sugar
¹/₂ cup vegetable oil
1 tablespoon finely chopped gingerroot or 1 teaspoon ground ginger
3 eggs
3 cups all-purpose flour
3¹/₂ teaspoons baking powder
1 teaspoon salt

Heat oven to 350°. Grease bottoms only of 2 loaf pans, 8¹/₂ × 4¹/₂ × 2¹/₂ or 9 × 5 × 3 inches. Mix pears, sugar, oil, gingerroot and eggs in large bowl. Stir in remaining ingredients. Pour into pans.

Bake 8-inch loaves about 65 minutes, 9-inch loaves about 50 minutes or until toothpick inserted in center comes out clean. Cool 10 minutes. Loosen sides of loaves from pans; remove from pans. Cool completely on wire rack before slicing. Store tightly wrapped in refrigerator up to 1 week. *2 loaves (24 slices each).*

Cardamom-Fig Bread

2¹/₂ cups all-purpose flour
1 cup sugar
1 cup chopped dried figs
1¹/₄ cups buttermilk
¹/₃ cup vegetable oil
1 teaspoon baking powder
¹/₂ teaspoon baking soda
¹/₂ teaspoon salt
¹/₂ teaspoon ground cardamom
2 eggs

Heat oven to 350°. Grease bottoms only of 2 loaf pans, 8¹/₂ × 4¹/₂ × 2¹/₂ inches, or 1 loaf pan, 9 × 5 × 3 inches. Mix all ingredients; beat 30 seconds. Pour into pans.

Bake 8-inch loaves 45 to 50 minutes, 9-inch loaf 55 to 60 minutes or until toothpick inserted in center comes out clean. Cool 10 minutes. Loosen sides of loaves from pans; remove from pans. Cool completely on wire rack before slicing. Store tightly wrapped in refrigerator up to 1 week. *2 loaves (12 slices each) or 1 loaf (24 slices).*

Chocolate-Pistachio Bread

²/₃ cup sugar
¹/₂ cup (1 stick) margarine or butter, melted
³/₄ cup milk
1 egg
1¹/₂ cups all-purpose flour
1 cup chopped pistachio nuts
¹/₂ cup semisweet chocolate chips
¹/₃ cup cocoa
2 teaspoons baking powder
¹/₄ teaspoon salt

Heat oven to 350°. Generously grease loaf pan, 8¹/₂ × 4¹/₂ × 2¹/₂ or 9 × 5 × 3 inches. Mix sugar, margarine, milk and egg in large bowl until well blended. Stir in remaining ingredients. Pour into pan. Sprinkle with sugar if desired.

Bake 50 to 55 minutes or until toothpick inserted in center comes out clean. Cool 10 minutes. Loosen sides of loaf from pan; remove from pan. Cool completely on wire rack before slicing. Store tightly wrapped in refrigerator up to 1 week. *1 loaf (24 slices).*

Marvelous Mini Loaves

Mini loaves or small breads in unusual shapes make wonderful treats. You can bake quick-bread batter in miniature loaf pans, muffin pans, small cake molds or other baking pans. Use these handy guidelines to turn your favorite banana, pumpkin or other fruit-and-nut bread into delightful little morsels!

- Measure the volume of pans by filling them to the top with water, then pouring the water into a measuring cup.
- Dry the pans well and grease them generously. Grease the bottoms only of muffin cups and miniature loaf pans. Thoroughly grease other pans, such as small cake molds.
- Spoon the batter into greased pans. Refer to the chart below to determine how much batter to spoon into each pan.
- Bake at 350° until a toothpick inserted in the center comes out clean. Use the chart below to determine approximate baking times. The dimensions and shapes of the pans will affect the baking time.
- Let the breads cool for a few minutes, then loosen the edges of the breads from the pans and carefully remove them from the pans. Cool completely on a wire rack.
- For a delicious gift, fill a basket with mini loaves wrapped in plastic wrap and tied with ribbons, a jar of jam, a few pretty napkins and some unusual coffees or teas.

Mini Loaves Baking Chart

Approximate Pan Volume	Amount of Batter	Approximate Baking Time
⅓ cup	¼ cup	15 to 20 minutes
½ cup	⅓ cup	15 to 20 minutes
⅔ to ¾ cup	½ cup	25 to 35 minutes
1 cup	¾ cup	35 to 40 minutes

Easy Brown Bread

1 cup all-purpose or rye flour
1 cup cornmeal
1 cup whole wheat flour
1 cup raisins, if desired
2 cups buttermilk
³/₄ cup molasses
2 teaspoons baking soda
¹/₂ teaspoon salt

Heat oven to 325°. Grease 2-quart casserole. Beat all ingredients in large bowl on low speed 30 seconds, scraping bowl constantly. Beat on medium speed 30 seconds, scraping bowl constantly. Pour into casserole. Bake about 1 hour or until loaf sounds hollow when tapped; remove from casserole. Cool on wire rack. *12 slices.*

Irish Soda Bread

3 tablespoons margarine or butter,
  softened
2¹/₂ cups all-purpose flour
2 tablespoons sugar
1 teaspoon baking soda
1 teaspoon baking powder
¹/₂ teaspoon salt
¹/₃ cup raisins
About ³/₄ cup buttermilk

Heat oven to 375°. Grease cookie sheet. Cut margarine into flour, sugar, baking soda, baking powder and salt in large bowl with pastry blender until mixture resembles fine crumbs. Stir in raisins. Stir in just enough buttermilk so dough leaves side of bowl.

Turn dough onto lightly floured surface; gently roll in flour to coat. Knead 1 to 2 minutes or until smooth. Shape into round loaf, about 6¹/₂ inches in diameter. Place on cookie sheet. Cut an X shape about ¹/₄ through loaf with floured knife. Bake 35 to 45 minutes or until golden brown. Remove from cookie sheet. Brush with softened margarine or butter if desired. Cool on wire rack. *8 slices.*

Pizza Loaf

If you love to sprinkle crushed red pepper on your pizza, you'll adore this savory bread! If the red pepper is too spicy for you, just leave it out.

Grated Parmesan cheese
1 cup milk
¼ cup olive or vegetable oil
2 teaspoons chopped fresh or ½ teaspoon dried basil leaves
¼ teaspoon crushed red pepper, if desired
1 egg
2¼ cups all-purpose flour
¾ cup shredded mozzarella cheese
⅓ cup chopped pepperoni
¼ cup sliced ripe olives
2 tablespoons grated Parmesan cheese
3 teaspoons baking powder

Heat oven to 350°. Generously grease loaf pan, 8½ × 4½ × 2½ or 9 × 5 × 3 inches; coat with Parmesan cheese. Mix milk, oil, basil, crushed red pepper and egg in large bowl. Stir in remaining ingredients. Spread in pan. Sprinkle with additional grated Parmesan cheese if desired.

Bake 45 to 50 minutes or until toothpick inserted in center comes out clean. Cool 5 minutes. Loosen sides and bottom of loaf from pan with flexible metal spatula; remove from pan. Cool on wire rack. Store tightly wrapped in refrigerator up to 2 days. *1 loaf (16 slices).*

Corn Bread

Try jazzing up this traditional favorite by stirring ½ cup shredded cheese, 1 can (4 ounces) chopped green chilies, drained, or 4 slices bacon, crisply cooked and crumbled, into the batter.

1½ cups cornmeal
½ cup all-purpose flour
1½ cups buttermilk
¼ cup vegetable oil
2 teaspoons baking powder
1 teaspoon sugar
1 teaspoon salt
½ teaspoon baking soda
2 eggs

Heat oven to 450°. Grease round pan, 9 × 1½ inches, square pan, 8 × 8 × 2 inches, or 10-inch ovenproof skillet. Mix all ingredients. Beat vigorously 30 seconds. Pour into pan. Bake round or square pan 25 to 30 minutes, skillet about 20 minutes or until golden brown. Serve warm. *8 or 9 pieces.*

Pizza Loaf

Easy Sausage–Corn Bread Loaf

You can tailor this recipe to be just as spicy as you like by choosing either a spicy or mild pork sausage.

> *³/₄ pound bulk pork sausage*
> *3 cups Bisquick Original baking mix*
> *1¹/₂ cups shredded Cheddar cheese (6 ounces)*
> *1 cup cornmeal*
> *1 cup milk*
> *2 tablespoons vegetable oil*
> *4 eggs*
> *2 medium tomatoes, seeded, chopped and drained (about 1¹/₂ cups)*

Heat oven to 375°. Grease bottom only of loaf pan, 9 × 5 × 3 inches; dust with baking mix. Cook sausage in 10-inch skillet over medium heat, stirring frequently, until brown. Drain if necessary. Cool sausage slightly; crumble. Mix sausage and remaining ingredients; beat 30 strokes. Spread in pan.

Bake 50 to 55 minutes or until toothpick inserted in center comes out clean. Cool 5 minutes. Loosen sides of loaf from pan; remove from pan. Cool on wire rack. Store tightly wrapped in refrigerator up to 2 days. *1 loaf (16 slices).*

Chipotle-Cheese Corn Bread

Choose hot, medium or mild chipotle chilies according to your taste.

> *1¹/₄ cups cornmeal*
> *³/₄ cup all-purpose flour*
> *¹/₂ cup shredded Monterey Jack cheese*
> *¹/₃ cup margarine or butter, melted*
> *1¹/₃ cups buttermilk*
> *1 tablespoon sugar*
> *2 teaspoons baking powder*
> *1 teaspoon salt*
> *¹/₂ teaspoon baking soda*
> *¹/₂ teaspoon ground cumin*
> *2 canned chipotle chilies in adobo sauce, chopped (about 1 tablespoon)*
> *2 eggs*

Heat oven to 450°. Grease round pan, 9 × 1¹/₂ inches, square pan, 8 × 8 × 2 inches, or 10-inch ovenproof skillet. Mix all ingredients; beat vigorously 30 seconds. Pour into pan. Bake round or square pan 25 to 30 minutes, skillet about 20 minutes or until golden brown. Serve warm. *8 or 9 pieces.*

Glazed Cinnamon-Raisin Batter Bread

Cinnamon-raisin bread is an all-time favorite. You'll love this recipe because it's easier and faster to make than ever!

> *3¹/₂ to 3³/₄ cups all-purpose flour*
> *2 tablespoons sugar*
> *1 teaspoon ground cinnamon*
> *¹/₂ teaspoon salt*
> *1 package regular or quick-acting active dry yeast*
> *1¹/₂ cups very warm water (120° to 130°)*
> *2 tablespoons margarine or butter, softened*
> *³/₄ cup raisins*
> *Glaze (right)*

Generously grease loaf pan, 8¹/₂ × 4¹/₂ × 2¹/₂ or 9 × 5 × 3 inches. Mix 2 cups of the flour, the sugar, cinnamon, salt and yeast in large bowl. Add warm water and margarine. Beat on low speed until moistened. Beat on medium speed 3 minutes, scraping bowl occasionally. Stir in raisins and enough remaining flour to make a stiff batter. Smooth and pat batter in pan with floured hands. Cover and let rise in warm place about 30 minutes or until batter is about ¹/₂ inch above top of 8-inch pan or about ¹/₂ inch below top of 9-inch pan.

Place oven rack in lowest position. Heat oven to 375°. Bake 45 to 50 minutes or until loaf is golden brown and sounds hollow when tapped; remove from pan. Cool completely on wire rack before slicing. Drizzle with Glaze. *1 loaf (16 slices).*

GLAZE

> *¹/₂ cup powdered sugar*
> *¹/₄ teaspoon vanilla*
> *2 to 2¹/₂ teaspoons milk*

Mix all ingredients until smooth and drizzling consistency.

Sensational Jams and Spreads

Make these easy jams, spreads and flavored butters to serve with your warm-from-the-oven breads. Try Blue Cheese Spread on English Muffin Bread (page 87), Strawberry Refrigerator Jam on Nut Bread (page 70) or Herbed Parmesan Butter on Potato-Tarragon Casserole Bread (page 87). Let your taste buds be your guide as you choose the spread or jam that's the perfect complement to your favorite homemade bread.

Strawberry Refrigerator Jam

2 packages (10 ounces each) frozen
   strawberries, thawed
1 package (1³/4 ounces) powdered
   fruit pectin
1 tablespoon grated orange peel
¹/2 cup orange juice
3¹/2 cups sugar

Mix strawberries, pectin, orange peel and orange juice in 3-quart saucepan until pectin is dissolved. Heat to rolling boil over high heat, stirring constantly. Stir in sugar. Heat to rolling boil, stirring constantly; remove from heat. Skim off foam. Immediately pour into freezer containers, leaving ¹/2-inch headspace. Seal immediately; cool. Refrigerate or freeze up to 3 months (thaw before serving). *About 4 half-pints jam.*

Pineapple-Apricot Refrigerator Jam

1 jar (6 ounces) maraschino cherries
1 can (20 ounces) crushed pineapple in
   heavy syrup, undrained
8 ounces dried apricots, cut into fourths
   (about 1 cup)
¹/4 cup water
3¹/2 cups sugar
2 tablespoons lemon juice
1 pouch (3 ounces) liquid fruit pectin

Drain cherries, reserving ¹/3 cup syrup. Chop cherries. Heat pineapple, reserved cherry syrup, the apricots and water to boiling in 4-quart Dutch oven, stirring occasionally; reduce heat. Cover and simmer about 10 minutes, stirring occasionally, until apricots are tender. Stir in sugar, lemon juice and cherries. Heat to rolling boil over high heat, stirring occasionally. Boil and stir 1 minute; remove from heat. Stir in pectin. Immediately pour into freezer containers, leaving ¹/2-inch headspace. Seal immediately; cool. Refrigerate or freeze up to 3 months (thaw before serving). *About 5 half-pints jam.*

Walnut Butter

*1 cup (2 sticks) margarine or butter,
  softened*
¹/₄ cup packed brown sugar
*¹/₂ cup chopped walnuts, toasted if
  desired (see page 47)*

Beat margarine and brown sugar in small
bowl on medium speed until fluffy. Stir in
walnuts. *About 1¹/₄ cups butter.*

——— ■ ———

Honey-Orange Butter

*1 cup (2 sticks) margarine or butter,
  softened*
2 tablespoons honey
2 teaspoons grated orange peel

Beat all ingredients on medium speed until
fluffy. *About 1 cup butter.*

——— ■ ———

Blue Cheese Spread

*2 packages (3 ounces each) cream
  cheese, softened*
2 ounces blue cheese, crumbled
2 teaspoons milk or half-and-half

Beat all ingredients on medium speed until
fluffy. *About 1 cup spread.*

Herbed Parmesan Butter

*¹/₂ cup (1 stick) margarine or butter,
  softened*
*2 tablespoons grated Parmesan
  cheese*
*1 teaspoon chopped fresh or ¹/₄ tea-
  spoon dried basil leaves*
*1 teaspoon chopped fresh or ¹/₄ tea-
  spoon dried marjoram leaves*

Beat all ingredients on medium speed until
fluffy. *About ²/₃ cup butter.*

——— ■ ———

Lemon–Cream Cheese Spread

*1 package (8 ounces) cream cheese,
  softened*
1 tablespoon powdered sugar
1 tablespoon lemon juice
1 teaspoon grated lemon peel

Beat all ingredients on medium speed until
fluffy. *About 1 cup spread.*

Chili-Cheese Batter Bread

You can substitute 1 cup of milk and 1 tablespoon vinegar for the buttermilk if need be.

2 cups all-purpose flour
2 teaspoons baking powder
³/4 teaspoon salt
¹/2 teaspoon baking soda
1 cup shredded Cheddar cheese (4 ounces)
1 can (4 ounces) chopped green chilies, well drained
1 cup buttermilk
1 tablespoon vegetable oil
1 egg

Heat oven to 350°. Grease pie plate, 9 × 1¹/4 inches. Mix flour, baking powder, salt and baking soda in large bowl. Add cheese and chilies; toss. Stir in remaining ingredients just until flour is moistened (batter will be lumpy). Pour into pie plate. Bake 40 to 45 minutes or until golden brown and toothpick inserted in center comes out clean; remove from pie plate. Cool on wire rack. *8 pieces.*

Fresh Herb Batter Bread

3 cups all-purpose flour
1 tablespoon sugar
1 teaspoon salt
1 package regular or quick-acting active dry yeast
1¹/4 cups very warm water (120° to 130°)
2 tablespoons chopped fresh parsley
2 tablespoons shortening
1¹/2 teaspoons chopped fresh or ¹/2 teaspoon dried rosemary leaves
¹/2 teaspoon chopped fresh or ¹/4 teaspoon dried thyme leaves
Margarine or butter, softened

Grease loaf pan, 9 × 5 × 3 inches. Mix 2 cups of the flour, the sugar, salt and yeast in large bowl. Add warm water, parsley, shortening, rosemary and thyme. Beat on low speed 1 minute, scraping bowl frequently. Beat on medium speed 1 minute, scraping bowl frequently. Stir in remaining flour until smooth. Smooth and pat batter in pan with floured hands. Cover and let rise in warm place about 40 minutes or until double.

Heat oven to 375°. Bake 40 to 45 minutes or until loaf sounds hollow when tapped; remove from pan. Brush with margarine. Cool on wire rack. *1 loaf (16 slices).*

Potato-Tarragon Casserole Bread

Casserole breads are no-knead yeast breads that are baked in casserole dishes. If you don't have any leftover mashed potatoes, prepare instant mashed potatoes as a quick alternative.

> *3¹/₂ cups all-purpose flour*
> *1 tablespoon chopped fresh or 1 tea-spoon dried tarragon leaves*
> *1 teaspoon salt*
> *1 package regular or quick-acting active dry yeast*
> *³/₄ cup very warm milk (120° to 130°)*
> *¹/₂ cup very warm water (120° to 130°)*
> *¹/₃ cup margarine or butter, softened*
> *1 egg*
> *³/₄ cup lukewarm mashed potatoes*

Grease 2-quart casserole. Mix 1½ cups of the flour, the tarragon, salt and yeast in large bowl. Add warm milk, warm water, margarine and egg. Beat on low speed 30 seconds, scraping bowl constantly. Beat on medium speed 2 minutes, scraping bowl occasionally. Stir in remaining flour and the potatoes. Spread evenly in casserole. Cover and let rise in warm place about 45 minutes or until double. (Batter is ready if indentation remains when touched with floured finger.)

Place oven rack in lowest position. Heat oven to 375°. Bake 45 to 50 minutes or until loaf is golden brown and sounds hollow when tapped; remove from casserole. Cool on wire rack. *12 slices.*

English Muffin Bread

> *Cornmeal*
> *2³/₄ cups all-purpose flour*
> *1 teaspoon salt*
> *1 teaspoon sugar*
> *1 package regular or quick-acting active dry yeast*
> *1 cup very warm water (120° to 130°)*
> *¹/₄ cup shortening*

Grease loaf pan, 8½ × 4½ × 2½ or 9 × 5 × 3 inches; coat with cornmeal. Mix 1½ cups of the flour, the salt, sugar and yeast in large bowl. Add warm water and shortening. Beat on low speed 30 seconds, scraping bowl constantly. Beat on high speed 3 minutes, scraping bowl occasionally. Stir in remaining flour. Smooth and pat batter in pan with floured hands. Sprinkle with cornmeal if desired. Cover and let rise in warm place about 45 minutes or until batter is about ¾ inch above top of 8-inch pan or about ¾ inch below top of 9-inch pan.

Heat oven to 375°. Bake 40 to 45 minutes or until loaf is golden brown and sounds hollow when tapped; remove from pan. Brush with softened margarine or butter if desired. Cool on wire rack. *1 loaf (16 slices).*

Cinnamon Crispies

¹/₂ cup (1 stick) margarine or butter
2 cups all-purpose flour
¹/₄ cup sugar
²/₃ cup milk
1 teaspoon baking powder
1 teaspoon salt
¹/₃ cup sugar
2 teaspoons ground cinnamon
Sugar

Heat oven to 425°. Grease 2 cookie sheets. Heat margarine until melted; reserve 2 tablespoons. Mix remaining margarine, the flour, ¹/₄ cup sugar, the milk, baking powder and salt in large bowl until dough forms. Turn dough onto lightly floured surface; gently roll in flour to coat. Knead lightly 10 times.

Divide dough in half. Roll or pat one half of dough into rectangle, 9 × 5 inches. Brush with half of reserved melted margarine. Mix ¹/₃ cup sugar and the cinnamon; sprinkle half over rectangle. Roll up tightly, beginning at 5-inch side. Pinch edge of dough into roll to seal. Cut roll into 4 equal pieces with sharp knife. Place cut sides up on cookie sheets; pat each into 6-inch circle. Sprinkle with sugar.

Bake 8 to 10 minutes or until edges are golden brown. Immediately remove from cookie sheets with metal spatula. Cool on wire rack. Repeat with remaining dough, melted margarine and cinnamon-sugar mixture. *8 crispies.*

Glazed Chocolate Oven Doughnuts

2¹/₃ cups Bisquick Original baking mix
¹/₄ cup sugar
¹/₂ cup milk
3 tablespoons cocoa
1 teaspoon vanilla
Chocolate Glaze (below)

Heat oven to 425°. Mix all ingredients except Chocolate Glaze until dough forms. Turn dough onto surface dusted with baking mix; gently roll in baking mix to coat. Knead lightly 10 times. Roll dough ¹/₂ inch thick. Cut with 2¹/₂-inch doughnut cutter. Place about 2 inches apart on ungreased cookie sheet.

Bake about 8 minutes or until set; remove from cookie sheet. Cool slightly on wire rack. Spread with Chocolate Glaze. Sprinkle with chopped nuts, coconut or multicolored candy shot if desired. *About 9 doughnuts.*

CHOCOLATE GLAZE

¹/₂ cup semisweet chocolate chips
1 tablespoon shortening

Heat ingredients in heavy 1-quart saucepan over low heat, stirring occasionally, until melted.

Cinnamon Crispies, Glazed Chocolate Oven Doughnuts

Bread Bowls

Yeast gives a terrific, slightly chewy texture to these fun bread bowls. Bowls filled with salad, chowder, chili or a thick stew are sure to be real crowd pleasers!

> *1 package regular or quick-acting active*
> * dry yeast*
> *¹/₄ cup warm water (105° to 115°)*
> *2 tablespoons sugar*
> *¹/₄ cup shortening*
> *3 cups all-purpose flour*
> *3 teaspoons baking powder*
> *³/₄ teaspoon salt*
> *About 1 cup buttermilk*

Dissolve yeast in warm water. Stir in sugar; reserve. Cut shortening into flour, baking powder and salt with pastry blender in large bowl until mixture resembles fine crumbs. Stir in yeast mixture and just enough buttermilk so dough leaves side of bowl and forms ball. Turn dough onto lightly floured surface; gently roll in flour to coat. Knead about 1 minute or until smooth. Cover and let rise 10 minutes.

Heat oven to 375°. Grease outsides of six 10-ounce custard cups. Place cups upside down on ungreased jelly roll pan, 15¹/₂ × 10¹/₂ × 1 inch. Divide dough into 6 equal parts. Pat or roll each part into 7-inch circle. Shape dough circles over outsides of custard cups. (Do not allow dough to curl under edges of cups.)

Bake 18 to 22 minutes or until golden brown. Carefully lift bread bowls from custard cups—custard cups and bread will be hot. Cool bread bowls upright on wire rack. *6 bread bowls.*

Cheesy Breadsticks

To make Cheesy Pretzels: roll each half of the dough into rectangle, 12 × 8 inches. Cut each rectangle lengthwise into 8 strips. Fold each strip lengthwise in half; pinch edges to seal. Twist folded strips into pretzel shapes; place seam sides down on greased cookie sheet. Brush pretzels with egg; sprinkle with the cheese mixture. Bake as directed.

> *¹/₄ cup grated Parmesan cheese*
> *¹/₂ teaspoon paprika*
> *2 cups all-purpose flour*
> *¹/₂ cup shredded Cheddar cheese*
> *³/₄ cup milk*
> *2 tablespoons margarine or butter,*
> * melted*
> *2 teaspoons baking powder*
> *1 teaspoon sugar*
> *1 teaspoon salt*
> *1 egg, beaten*

Mix Parmesan cheese and paprika; reserve. Mix remaining ingredients except egg until dough leaves side of bowl. Turn dough onto lightly floured surface; gently roll in flour to coat. Knead lightly 20 to 25 times. Cover and let stand 15 minutes.

Heat oven to 400°. Grease 2 cookie sheets. Divide dough in half. Cover and reserve one-half of dough. Roll other half of dough into rectangle, 10 × 8 inches. Brush with half of the egg; sprinkle with half of the cheese mixture. Press cheese mixture lightly into dough. Cut rectangle lengthwise into 12 strips. Gently twist each strip several times; place on one of the cookie sheets.

Bake 12 to 15 minutes or until golden brown. Immediately remove from cookie sheet. Cool on wire rack. Repeat with remaining dough, egg and cheese mixture. *24 breadsticks.*

Bread Bowls, Cheesy Breadsticks

5
Good-for-You Breads

Healthful coffee cakes, muffins and biscuits *are* possible—and they're delicious, too. We wanted to devote an entire chapter to recipes that keep fat to a minimum and emphasize healthful ingredients such as whole grains and fruit. You may want to bake something special but then think, "It's too high in calories or has too much cholesterol." Well, these recipes are just for you.

You'll see grains that might be unfamiliar in some of these recipes. But they're not to be missed! Page 98 explains what each of these grains is, and there's a photo to show you what each of them looks like. Be sure to try them; you'll love the new flavors and textures. On pages 108–109 we show you how to make your favorite recipes more healthful by cutting down on sugar and fat.

Nutrition information is included for each of these recipes. It includes the amount of calories, protein, carbohydrate, fat, cholesterol, sodium and fiber. The percent of U.S. RDA is indicated for vitamin A, vitamin C, thiamin, riboflavin, niacin, calcium and iron. The U.S. RDAs are set by the Food and Drug Administration and are based on the needs of most healthy adults. As you review the nutrition information, keep these things in mind:

- If a choice of ingredients is given ("1 cup plain low-fat or nonfat yogurt," for example), note that the first choice was used in nutrition information calculations.
- If a range of ingredients is given ("2 to 3 teaspoons skim milk," for example), the first amount was used in nutrition information calculations.
- "If desired" ingredients ("Sprinkle with sugar if desired") were not included in nutrition information calculations.
- An asterisk (*) indicates U.S. RDA levels of less than 2%.

Fruity Multigrain Muffins (page 94)

93

Spicy Apple-Bran Muffins

1 cup plain low-fat or nonfat yogurt
*1 cup chopped peeled or unpeeled apple
    (about 1 medium)*
*¼ cup frozen (thawed) apple juice
    concentrate*
3 tablespoons vegetable oil
*3 egg whites or ¼ cup cholesterol-free
    egg product*
1 cup all-purpose flour
1 cup oat bran
¼ cup granulated sugar
3 teaspoons baking powder
¾ teaspoon ground cinnamon
¼ teaspoon salt
¼ teaspoon ground nutmeg
1 tablespoon packed brown sugar

Heat oven to 400°. Spray 12 medium muffin cups, 2½ × 1¼ inches, with nonstick cooking spray, or line with paper baking cups. Beat yogurt, apple, apple juice concentrate, oil and egg whites in large bowl. Stir in remaining ingredients except brown sugar just until flour is moistened. Divide batter evenly among muffin cups (cups will be almost full). Sprinkle with brown sugar. Bake 20 to 24 minutes or until golden brown. Immediately remove from pan. *12 muffins.*

Nutrition Information Per Serving

1 muffin		% of U.S. RDA	
Calories	150	Vitamin A	*
Protein, g	4	Vitamin C	*
Carbohydrate, g	24	Thiamin	12%
Fat, g	4	Riboflavin	8%
Cholesterol, mg	0	Niacin	4%
Sodium, mg	170	Calcium	10%
Fiber, g	2	Iron	6%

Fruity Multigrain Muffins

1¼ cups plain low-fat or nonfat yogurt
½ cup packed brown sugar
¼ cup vegetable oil
2 egg whites
1¼ cups whole wheat flour
¾ cup oat bran
*¼ cup stone-ground or degerminated
    cornmeal (see page 111)*
1 teaspoon baking powder
½ teaspoon baking soda
¼ teaspoon salt
*½ cup chopped dried fruit (apricots,
    peaches, apples or figs)*
*½ cup cooked whole-grain triticale (see
    page 98) or brown rice*

Heat oven to 400°. Spray 12 medium muffin cups, 2½ × 1¼ inches, with nonstick cooking spray, or line with paper baking cups. Beat yogurt, brown sugar, oil and egg whites in large bowl. Stir in remaining ingredients except dried fruit and triticale just until flour is moistened. Fold in dried fruit and triticale. Divide batter evenly among muffin cups (cups will be very full). Sprinkle with brown sugar if desired. Bake 20 to 22 minutes or until golden brown. Immediately remove from pan. *12 muffins.*

Nutrition Information Per Serving

1 muffin		% of U.S. RDA	
Calories	205	Vitamin A	14%
Protein, g	5	Vitamin C	*
Carbohydrate, g	33	Thiamin	8%
Fat, g	6	Riboflavin	6%
Cholesterol, mg	0	Niacin	4%
Sodium, mg	160	Calcium	8%
Fiber, g	3	Iron	8%

Carrot-Buckwheat Muffins

Buckwheat flour is best combined with whole wheat or all-purpose flour. If you don't have buckwheat flour, you can use ½ cup all-purpose flour or whole wheat flour instead in this recipe.

½ cup boiling water
¼ cup uncooked buckwheat groats†
*   (kasha); (see page 98)*
½ cup packed brown sugar
½ cup skim milk
¼ cup vegetable oil
2 tablespoons molasses
3 egg whites
1½ cups whole wheat flour
½ cup buckwheat flour
3 teaspoons baking powder
½ teaspoon salt
½ teaspoon ground cinnamon
¼ teaspoon ground cloves
1 cup shredded carrots (about 2 medium)

Pour boiling water over buckwheat groats in small bowl. Cover and let stand 10 minutes or until water is absorbed; reserve.

Heat oven to 400°. Spray 12 medium muffin cups, 2½ × 1¼ inches, with nonstick cooking spray, or line with paper baking cups. Beat brown sugar, milk, oil, molasses and egg whites in large bowl. Stir in remaining ingredients except carrots just until flour is moistened. Fold in carrots and buckwheat groats. Divide batter evenly among muffin cups (cups will be very full). Bake 22 to 24 minutes or until golden brown. Immediately remove from pan. *12 muffins.*

†½ cup uncooked quick-cooking brown rice can be substituted for the buckwheat groats. Decrease boiling water to ¼ cup.

Nutrition Information Per Serving

1 muffin		% of U.S. RDA	
Calories	175	Vitamin A	14%
Protein, g	4	Vitamin C	*
Carbohydrate, g	29	Thiamin	6%
Fat, g	5	Riboflavin	6%
Cholesterol, mg	0	Niacin	6%
Sodium, mg	210	Calcium	10%
Fiber, g	2	Iron	8%

Triple Wheat-Blueberry Muffins

Lower-fat muffins tend to stick to paper baking cups. Therefore, you might want to use muffin cups sprayed with nonstick cooking spray instead of paper baking cups.

1¼ cups low-fat or nonfat buttermilk
⅓ cup honey
¼ cup vegetable oil
1 teaspoon vanilla
2 egg whites
1¼ cups whole wheat flour
1 cup toasted wheat bran
1 teaspoon baking powder
½ teaspoon baking soda
½ teaspoon salt
¼ teaspoon ground nutmeg
1 cup fresh or frozen (thawed and drained) blueberries
¾ cup cooked whole-grain wheat (see page 98) or brown rice

Heat oven to 400°. Spray 12 medium muffin cups, 2½ × 1¼ inches, with nonstick cooking spray, or line with paper baking cups. Beat buttermilk, honey, oil, vanilla and egg whites in large bowl. Stir in flour, wheat bran, baking powder, baking soda, salt and nutmeg just until flour is moistened. Fold in blueberries and whole-grain wheat. Divide batter evenly among muffin cups (cups will be very full). Bake 22 to 24 minutes or until golden brown. Immediately remove from pan. *12 muffins.*

Nutrition Information Per Serving

1 muffin		% of U.S. RDA	
Calories	160	Vitamin A	*
Protein, g	4	Vitamin C	*
Carbohydrate, g	25	Thiamin	6%
Fat, g	5	Riboflavin	8%
Cholesterol, mg	0	Niacin	8%
Sodium, mg	230	Calcium	6%
Fiber, g	4	Iron	6%

Triple Wheat-Blueberry Muffins, Pumpkin-Fruit Bread (page 109)

Good-For-You Grains

Look for nutritious and inexpensive whole grains in supermarkets, co-ops and health food stores. They provide B vitamins, iron, complex carbohydrates and dietary fiber. For nutritious and delicious muffins, coffee cakes and other baked goods, try adding cooked whole grains to batters and doughs.

Amaranth is a poppy-seed–size grain, containing iron, phosphorous and complex carbohydrates. It is golden in color with an occasional dark seed.

Barley contains niacin, thiamin and potassium. Hulled or Scotch barley is produced by removing the hull and some of the bran. Pearl barley, the form most commonly available, has had the hull, most of the bran and some of the germ removed.

Buckwheat kernels, or groats, are hulled seeds of the buckwheat plant. Although buckwheat is technically a fruit, it is cooked and served like a grain. Roasted buckwheat groats are often called kasha. Buckwheat contains phosphorous, iron, potassium and B vitamins.

Bulgur is whole wheat that's been cooked, dried and then broken into coarse fragments. It's different from cracked wheat because it is precooked. Bulgur contains phosphorus, potassium, iron, thiamin and riboflavin.

Cracked wheat is whole wheat kernels that have been dried and then cracked by coarse milling. Like bulgur (its precooked cousin), cracked wheat contains phosphorus, potassium, iron, thiamin and riboflavin.

Oats, well known for their fiber content, contain thiamin, phosphorus and magnesium. The oats commonly eaten as breakfast cereal are oat kernels that have been steamed and flattened. Oat bran is broken husks of oat kernels.

Quinoa provides B vitamins, calcium, iron and phosphorus. Each cream-colored, round grain is only about $1/16$ inch in diameter. Unlike other grains, it contains complete protein. Be sure to rinse quinoa well before using it to remove the bitter-tasting, naturally occurring saponin—nature's insect repellent.

Teff is a reddish brown seed and the smallest of all grains. It contains complex carbohydrates, iron and fiber. The consistency of cooked teff is similar to that of stiff cornmeal mush.

Triticale is a hybrid of wheat and rye that contains more protein than either of its parents. Triticale berries resemble wheat berries, but they are a bit larger.

Whole-grain wheat, also called wheat berries, is unprocessed whole wheat. It contains B vitamins and complex carbohydrates. Cooked wheat berries can be used like rice in side dishes.

Wild rice is actually the seed of an aquatic grass. It contains protein (more than is found in true grains), fiber, B vitamins, iron, phosphorus, magnesium, calcium and zinc.

Cooking Grains

Grains vary in cooking times and the amounts of water needed. When making recipes that call for cooked grains, follow cooking directions on the grain package. If you purchase grains in bulk, ask for cooking directions where you buy the grains. Keep these things in mind:

- Most grains should be rinsed well in water before cooking. Use a strainer with an extrafine mesh when rinsing small grains such as quinoa and teff.
- Grains become drier with age, so the amount of water needed for cooking varies. If all the water is absorbed but the grain isn't tender, add a little more liquid and cook a little longer. If it's tender but all the water isn't absorbed, drain the grain.
- Cooked grains can be covered and refrigerated for about one week.
- If you have more of a cooked grain than you need for a recipe, add some to a casserole in place of some of the meat, or toss with vegetables for a hearty side dish.

Wheat bran *Rolled wheat* *Cracked wheat* *Bulgur* *Whole-grain wheat*

Rolled oats *Oat bran* *Wild rice* *Barley* *Buckwheat*

Cornmeal *Amaranth* *Triticale* *Quinoa* *Teff*

Ricotta-Spinach Muffins

½ cup low-fat ricotta cheese
¼ cup (½ stick) margarine, melted
¾ cup skim milk
2 egg whites
1 cup all-purpose flour
½ cup whole wheat flour
½ cup rolled wheat or regular oats
*½ cup coarsely chopped fresh or ¼ cup
    thawed, very well drained frozen
    spinach*
2 tablespoons grated Parmesan cheese
2½ teaspoons baking powder
¼ teaspoon salt

Heat oven to 400°. Spray 8 medium muffin cups, 2½ × 1¼ inches, with nonstick cooking spray, or line with paper baking cups. Beat ricotta cheese, margarine, milk and egg whites in large bowl. Stir in remaining ingredients just until flour is moistened. Divide batter evenly among muffin cups (cups will be very full). Sprinkle with additional grated Parmesan cheese if desired. Bake 22 to 24 minutes or until golden brown. Immediately remove from pan. *8 muffins.*

Nutrition Information Per Serving

1 muffin		% of U.S. RDA	
Calories	195	Vitamin A	14%
Protein, g	7	Vitamin C	*
Carbohydrate, g	24	Thiamin	12%
Fat, g	8	Riboflavin	12%
Cholesterol, mg	5	Niacin	8%
Sodium, mg	400	Calcium	18%
Fiber, g	2	Iron	8%

Parmesan-Barley Muffins

You can use either pearl barley or quick-cooking barley in these delicious muffins. Follow directions on the package for cooking barley.

1¼ cups skim milk
¼ cup vegetable oil
1 tablespoon chopped fresh or 1 teaspoon dried basil leaves
2 egg whites
2 cups whole wheat flour
¼ cup grated Parmesan cheese
2½ teaspoons baking powder
½ teaspoon salt
¾ cup cooked barley (see page 98)

Heat oven to 400°. Spray 12 medium muffin cups, 2½ × 1¼ inches, with nonstick cooking spray, or line with paper baking cups. Beat milk, oil, basil and egg whites in large bowl. Stir in remaining ingredients except barley just until flour is moistened. Fold in barley. Divide batter evenly among muffin cups (cups will be very full). Bake 20 to 22 minutes or until golden brown. Immediately remove from pan. *12 muffins.*

Nutrition Information Per Serving

1 muffin		% of U.S. RDA	
Calories	150	Vitamin A	2%
Protein, g	5	Vitamin C	*
Carbohydrate, g	19	Thiamin	6%
Fat, g	6	Riboflavin	6%
Cholesterol, mg	0	Niacin	6%
Sodium, mg	230	Calcium	12%
Fiber, g	2	Iron	4%

Hearty Multigrain Biscuits

You can expect these biscuits (and other breads made with whole grains) to be a little lower in volume than traditional biscuits.

¼ cup shortening
¾ cup whole wheat flour
½ cup all-purpose flour
*½ cup stone-ground or degerminated
     cornmeal (see page 111)*
3 teaspoons baking powder
½ teaspoon salt
½ cup quick-cooking or regular oats
About ¾ cup skim milk

Heat oven to 450°. Cut shortening into whole wheat flour, all-purpose flour, cornmeal, baking powder and salt with pastry blender in large bowl until mixture resembles fine crumbs. Stir in oats. Stir in just enough milk so dough leaves side of bowl and forms a ball.

Turn dough onto lightly floured surface; gently roll in flour to coat. Knead lightly 10 times. Roll or pat ½ inch thick. Cut with floured 2½-inch biscuit cutter. Place about 1 inch apart on ungreased cookie sheet. Brush with milk and sprinkle with oats if desired. Bake 10 to 12 minutes or until golden brown. Immediately remove from cookie sheet. Serve hot. *About 10 biscuits.*

Nutrition Information Per Serving

1 biscuit		% of U.S. RDA	
Calories	150	Vitamin A	*
Protein, g	3	Vitamin C	*
Carbohydrate, g	21	Thiamin	12%
Fat, g	6	Riboflavin	6%
Cholesterol, mg	0	Niacin	6%
Sodium, mg	230	Calcium	10%
Fiber, g	2	Iron	6%

Bulgur Biscuits

1/4 cup shortening
1 cup all-purpose flour
1 cup whole wheat flour
3 teaspoons baking powder
1/2 teaspoon salt
1/2 cup cooked bulgur (see page 98) or
  brown rice
About 2/3 cup skim milk

Heat oven to 450°. Cut shortening into flours, baking powder and salt with pastry blender in large bowl until mixture resembles fine crumbs. Stir in bulgur. Stir in just enough milk so dough leaves side of bowl and forms a ball.

Turn dough onto lightly floured surface; gently roll in flour to coat. Knead lightly 10 times. Roll or pat 1/2 inch thick. Cut with floured 2½-inch biscuit cutter. Place about 1 inch apart on ungreased cookie sheet. Bake 12 to 14 minutes or until golden brown. Immediately remove from cookie sheet. Serve hot. *About 10 biscuits.*

Nutrition Information Per Serving

1 biscuit		% of U.S. RDA	
Calories	150	Vitamin A	*
Protein, g	3	Vitamin C	*
Carbohydrate, g	21	Thiamin	10%
Fat, g	6	Riboflavin	6%
Cholesterol, mg	0	Niacin	8%
Sodium, mg	280	Calcium	10%
Fiber, g	2	Iron	6%

Sour Cream Biscuits

2 tablespoons firm margarine
1³/4 cups all-purpose flour
2¹/2 teaspoons baking powder
1/4 teaspoon salt
1/2 cup reduced-fat sour cream
1/3 cup skim milk

Heat oven to 450°. Cut margarine into flour, baking powder and salt with pastry blender in large bowl until mixture resembles fine crumbs. Mix sour cream and milk until smooth. Stir sour cream mixture into flour mixture until dough leaves side of bowl and forms a ball.

Turn dough onto lightly floured surface; gently roll in flour to coat. Knead lightly 10 times. Roll or pat 1/2 inch thick. Cut with floured 2½-inch biscuit cutter. Place about 1 inch apart on ungreased cookie sheet. Bake 10 to 12 minutes or until golden brown. Immediately remove from cookie sheet. Serve hot. *About 8 biscuits.*

Nutrition Information Per Serving

1 biscuit		% of U.S. RDA	
Calories	150	Vitamin A	6%
Protein, g	4	Vitamin C	*
Carbohydrate, g	24	Thiamin	16%
Fat, g	4	Riboflavin	10%
Cholesterol, mg	5	Niacin	8%
Sodium, mg	240	Calcium	10%
Fiber, g	1	Iron	6%

Bulgur Biscuits

Buttermilk–Toasted Oat Scones

Whole grains absorb liquid differently than all-purpose flour, so be careful not to add too much liquid to these scones.

½ cup quick-cooking or regular oats
½ cup oat bran
3 tablespoons firm margarine
1 cup all-purpose flour
¼ cup packed brown sugar
1½ teaspoons baking powder
¼ teaspoon baking soda
¼ teaspoon salt
½ cup chopped figs or prunes
2 egg whites
About ½ cup low-fat or nonfat buttermilk

Heat oven to 350°. Spread oats and oat bran in ungreased rectangular pan, 13 × 9 × 2 inches. Bake 15 to 20 minutes, stirring occasionally, until light brown; cool.

Increase oven temperature to 400°. Cut margarine into flour, brown sugar, baking powder, baking soda and salt with pastry blender in large bowl until mixture resembles fine crumbs. Stir in oat mixture and figs. Stir in egg whites and just enough buttermilk so dough leaves side of bowl and forms a ball.

Turn dough onto lightly floured surface; gently roll in flour to coat. Knead lightly 10 times. Pat or roll into 8-inch circle on ungreased cookie sheet. Cut into 8 wedges, but do not separate. Brush with buttermilk and sprinkle with oats if desired. Bake 16 to 18 minutes or until golden brown. Immediately remove from cookie sheet; carefully separate wedges. Serve warm. *8 scones.*

Nutrition Information Per Serving

1 scone		% of U.S. RDA	
Calories	180	Vitamin A	6%
Protein, g	5	Vitamin C	*
Carbohydrate, g	29	Thiamin	16%
Fat, g	5	Riboflavin	10%
Cholesterol, mg	0	Niacin	4%
Sodium, mg	250	Calcium	8%
Fiber, g	2	Iron	8%

To cut scones into diamond shapes as shown in the photograph, pat dough into an 8-inch diamond. Cut that into 9 smaller diamonds.

Buttermilk–Toasted Oat Scones

Citrus-Currant Scones

¹/₄ cup sugar
2 teaspoons grated lemon or orange
   peel
3 tablespoons firm margarine
1³/₄ cups all-purpose flour
2¹/₂ teaspoons baking powder
¹/₄ teaspoon salt
¹/₃ cup plain low-fat or nonfat yogurt
3 egg whites, slightly beaten
¹/₂ cup currants or raisins
Skim milk

Heat oven to 375°. Mix sugar and lemon peel; reserve 1 tablespoon. Cut margarine into remaining sugar mixture, the flour, baking powder and salt with pastry blender in large bowl until mixture resembles fine crumbs. Stir in yogurt, egg whites and currants until dough leaves side of bowl and forms a ball.

Turn dough onto lightly floured surface; gently roll in flour to coat. Knead lightly 10 times. Pat or roll into 8-inch circle on ungreased cookie sheet. Cut into 8 wedges, but do not separate. Brush with milk. Sprinkle with reserved sugar mixture. Bake 18 to 20 minutes or until edge is light brown. Immediately remove from cookie sheet; carefully separate wedges. Serve warm. *8 scones.*

Nutrition Information Per Serving

1 scone		% of U.S. RDA	
Calories	210	Vitamin A	6%
Protein, g	5	Vitamin C	*
Carbohydrate, g	36	Thiamin	16%
Fat, g	5	Riboflavin	14%
Cholesterol, mg	0	Niacin	8%
Sodium, mg	270	Calcium	10%
Fiber, g	1	Iron	8%

Honey–Whole Wheat Scones

¹/₄ cup (¹/₂ stick) firm margarine
2 cups whole wheat flour
2 teaspoons baking powder
¹/₂ teaspoon ground cinnamon
¹/₄ teaspoon salt
¹/₃ cup plain low-fat or nonfat yogurt
¹/₄ cup honey
3 egg whites, slightly beaten
1 tablespoon uncooked cracked wheat
   (see page 98)

Heat oven to 375°. Spray cookie sheet lightly with nonstick cooking spray. Cut margarine into flour, baking powder, cinnamon and salt with pastry blender in large bowl until mixture resembles fine crumbs. Stir in yogurt, honey and egg whites until dough leaves side of bowl and forms a ball.

Turn dough onto lightly floured surface; gently roll in flour to coat. Knead lightly 10 times. Pat or roll into 8-inch circle on cookie sheet with floured hands. Cut into 8 wedges, but do not separate. Sprinkle with cracked wheat; press lightly into dough. Bake 19 to 21 minutes or until edge is light brown. Immediately remove from cookie sheet; carefully separate wedges. Serve warm. *8 scones.*

Nutrition Information Per Serving

1 scone		% of U.S. RDA	
Calories	205	Vitamin A	8%
Protein, g	6	Vitamin C	*
Carbohydrate, g	32	Thiamin	10%
Fat, g	6	Riboflavin	8%
Cholesterol, mg	0	Niacin	10%
Sodium, mg	260	Calcium	8%
Fiber, g	3	Iron	6%

Banana Bread

2/3 cup sugar
1/4 cup (1/2 stick) margarine, softened
1 cup mashed ripe bananas (about 2 medium)
1/4 cup water
1 egg
2 egg whites
1 2/3 cups all-purpose flour
1 teaspoon baking soda
1/2 teaspoon salt
1/4 teaspoon baking powder

Heat oven to 350°. Spray loaf pan, 8½ × 4½ × 2½ or 9 × 5 × 3 inches, with nonstick cooking spray. Beat sugar and margarine in medium bowl on medium speed about 30 seconds, scraping bowl constantly, until light and fluffy. Beat in bananas, water, egg and egg whites on low speed about 30 seconds or until well blended. Stir in remaining ingredients just until moistened. Pour into pan.

Bake 8-inch loaf about 60 minutes, 9-inch loaf 45 to 50 minutes or until toothpick inserted in center comes out clean. Cool 5 minutes. Loosen sides of loaf from pan; remove from pan. Cool completely on wire rack before slicing. Store tightly wrapped in refrigerator up to 1 week. *1 loaf (24 slices).*

Nutrition Information Per Serving

1 slice		% of U.S. RDA	
Calories	80	Vitamin A	2%
Protein, g	1	Vitamin C	*
Carbohydrate, g	14	Thiamin	4%
Fat, g	2	Riboflavin	4%
Cholesterol, mg	10	Niacin	2%
Sodium, mg	110	Calcium	*
Fiber, g	0	Iron	2%

Zucchini-Apricot Bread

1½ cups shredded zucchini (about 1½ medium)
3/4 cup sugar
1/4 cup vegetable oil
3 egg whites or 1/2 cup cholesterol-free egg product
1½ cups all-purpose flour
1 teaspoon ground cinnamon
2 teaspoons vanilla
3/4 teaspoon baking soda
1/2 teaspoon salt
1/4 teaspoon baking powder
1/4 teaspoon ground cloves
1/2 cup finely chopped dried apricots

Heat oven to 350°. Spray loaf pan, 8½ × 4½ × 2½ or 9 × 5 × 3 inches, with nonstick cooking spray. Mix zucchini, sugar, oil and egg whites in large bowl. Stir in remaining ingredients except apricots. Stir in the apricots. Pour into pan.

Bake 60 to 70 minutes or until toothpick inserted in center comes out clean. Cool 10 minutes. Loosen sides of loaf from pan; remove from pan. Cool completely on wire rack before slicing. Store tightly wrapped in refrigerator up to 1 week. *1 loaf (24 slices).*

Nutrition Information Per Serving

1 slice		% of U.S. RDA	
Calories	80	Vitamin A	2%
Protein, g	1	Vitamin C	*
Carbohydrate, g	14	Thiamin	4%
Fat, g	2	Riboflavin	4%
Cholesterol, mg	0	Niacin	2%
Sodium, mg	80	Calcium	*
Fiber, g	0	Iron	2%

Good-for-You Recipe Makeover

Healthful eating doesn't mean you have to give up your favorite muffins, biscuits and coffee cakes. By making a few simple changes to a recipe, you can increase its nutritional value significantly. Here are a few guidelines for making mouth-watering baked goods with less fat, cholesterol, sugar and sodium and more fiber:

- When reducing fat in recipes, decrease it gradually until desired results are achieved. For example, on the first test for Pumpkin-Fruit Bread (right), we decreased the oil from ⅓ cup to ¼ cup. Because the loaf was still moist and tender, we tested it with 3 tablespoons oil. Again, the loaf was moist and tender, so we decreased the oil to 2 tablespoons. The resulting loaf was a little dry, so we wrote the final recipe with 3 tablespoons oil. Follow the same steps when reducing sugar.
- Use the chart below to substitute egg whites for whole eggs, or use ¼ cup cholesterol-free egg product for each whole egg. Some brands of cholesterol-free egg product contain fat while others do not. Read package labels to choose the brand that meets your needs.

Instead of	Use
1 egg	2 egg whites
2 eggs	3 egg whites
3 eggs	5 egg whites
4 eggs	6 egg whites

- Try substituting cooked whole grains and dried fruits for chopped nuts in baked goods. Grains and fruits add texture and flavor, but they contain no fat and fewer calories than nuts. If you must have nuts, use fewer and chop them finely. Because smaller pieces will be more evenly distributed through the batter than larger ones, you might not even miss the nuts you've left out.
- Replace some or all of the all-purpose flour with whole wheat flour to add fiber. To start, we suggest replacing half of the all-purpose flour with whole wheat flour. If you like the results, substitute whole wheat flour for more of the all-purpose flour next time. Doughs and batters made with whole wheat flour will be a little thicker and darker.
- If you're concerned about sodium in your diet, gradually cut back on the amount of salt used in baked goods, which usually contain a little salt to bring out the flavor. Recipes made with yeast need salt to prevent excessive rising of the dough. Do not eliminate salt in these recipes.

We used these guidelines to turn our traditional Pumpkin Bread into delicious, low-fat Pumpkin-Fruit Bread. Just look at the difference a few changes made!

Pumpkin-Fruit Bread

1 cup canned pumpkin
²/₃ cup packed brown sugar
3 tablespoons vegetable oil
1 teaspoon vanilla
3 egg whites or ¹/₂ cup cholesterol-free
    egg product
1¹/₂ cups all-purpose flour
¹/₂ cup diced dried fruit and raisin
    mixture
2 teaspoons baking powder
¹/₂ teaspoon salt
³/₄ teaspoon ground cinnamon
¹/₄ teaspoon ground cloves

Heat oven to 350°. Spray loaf pan, 9 × 5 × 3 or 8¹/₂ × 4¹/₂ × 2¹/₂ inches, with nonstick cooking spray. mix pumpkin, brown sugar, oil, vanilla and egg whites in large bowl. Stir in remaining ingredients just until moistened. Pour into pan.

Bake 50 to 60 minutes or until toothpick inserted in center comes out clean. Cool 5 minutes. Loosen sides of loaf from pan; remove from pan. Cool completely on wire rack before slicing. Store tightly wrapped in refrigerator up to 1 week. *1 loaf (24 slices).*

Nutrition Information Per Serving

1 slice		% of U.S. RDA	
Calories	80	Vitamin A	22%
Protein, g	1	Vitamin C	*
Carbohydrate, g	15	Thiamin	4%
Fat, g	2	Riboflavin	4%
Cholesterol, mg	0	Niacin	2%
Sodium, mg	100	Calcium	2%
Fiber, g	0	Iron	4%

Makeover Results

Change	Calories Saved	Fat Saved (g)	Cholesterol Saved (mg)
²/₃ cup sugar instead of 1 cup	263	0	0
3 tablespoons vegetable oil instead of ¹/₃ cup	280	32	0
3 egg whites replace 2 whole eggs	99	12	426
Mixed dried fruit replaces chopped walnuts	185	37	0
Total Savings	827	81	426
Savings per slice	35	4	18

Wild Rice–Amaranth Bread

¹/₄ cup uncooked wild rice
1¹/₄ cups water
¹/₂ cup uncooked amaranth† (see page 98)
¹/₂ cup packed brown sugar
1 cup skim milk
¹/₄ cup vegetable oil
¹/₄ cup honey
3 egg whites
1¹/₂ cups whole wheat flour
1 cup all-purpose flour
3 teaspoons baking powder
¹/₂ teaspoon salt

Rinse wild rice; drain. Heat wild rice and water to boiling in heavy 1¹/₂-quart saucepan; reduce heat. Cover and simmer 30 minutes. Stir in amaranth. Cover and simmer about 20 minutes longer or until water is absorbed. After 10 minutes, check to see that mixture is not sticking to the pan. Stir in 1 to 2 tablespoons water if mixture is sticking. Cool 10 minutes.

Heat oven to 350°. Spray 2 loaf pans, 8¹/₂ × 4¹/₂ × 2¹/₂ inches, or 1 loaf pan, 9 × 5 × 3 inches, with nonstick cooking spray. Mix wild rice mixture, brown sugar, milk, oil, honey and egg whites in large bowl. Stir in remaining ingredients. Pour into pans.

Bake 45 to 55 minutes or until toothpick inserted in center comes out clean. Cool 5 minutes. Loosen sides of loaves from pans; remove from pans. Cool completely on wire rack before slicing. Store tightly wrapped in refrigerator up to 1 week. *2 loaves (12 slices each) or 1 loaf (24 slices).*

†If you can't find amaranth, increase wild rice to ³/₄ cup and water to 1³/₄ cups. Heat wild rice and water to boiling as directed above, and simmer 40 to 50 minutes or until wild rice is tender. Do not use 9 × 5 × 3-inch loaf pan.

Nutrition Information Per Serving

1 slice		% of U.S. RDA	
Calories	125	Vitamin A	*
Protein, g	3	Vitamin C	*
Carbohydrate, g	21	Thiamin	4%
Fat, g	3	Riboflavin	4%
Cholesterol, mg	0	Niacin	4%
Sodium, mg	110	Calcium	4%
Fiber, g	1	Iron	10%

Honey-Raisin Wheat Bread

³/₄ cup cooked cracked wheat (see page 98)
1¹/₄ cups skim milk
¹/₂ cup honey
¹/₄ cup vegetable oil
1 teaspoon vanilla
1 egg
2³/₄ cups whole wheat flour
3 teaspoons baking powder
¹/₂ teaspoon salt
³/₄ cup raisins

Heat oven to 350°. Spray bottom only of 1 loaf pan, 9 × 5 × 3 inches, or 2 loaf pans, 8¹/₂ × 4¹/₂ × 2¹/₂ inches, with nonstick cooking spray. Mix cracked wheat, milk, honey, oil, vanilla and egg in large bowl. Stir in flour, baking powder and salt. Stir in raisins. Pour into pan.

Bake 9-inch loaf 55 to 60 minutes, 8-inch loaves 40 to 45 minutes or until toothpick inserted in center comes out clean. Cool 10 minutes. Loosen sides of loaf from pan; remove from pan. Cool completely on wire rack before slicing. Store tightly wrapped in refrigerator up to 1 week. *1 loaf (24 slices) or 2 loaves (12 slices each).*

Nutrition Information Per Serving

1 slice		% of U.S. RDA	
Calories	130	Vitamin A	*
Protein, g	3	Vitamin C	*
Carbohydrate, g	23	Thiamin	6%
Fat, g	3	Riboflavin	4%
Cholesterol, mg	10	Niacin	6%
Sodium, mg	105	Calcium	4%
Fiber, g	2	Iron	4%

Quinoa Corn Bread

Stone-ground cornmeal contains the bran and germ from the corn kernels, so it gives bread a coarse texture and a grainy flavor. Degerminated cornmeal has had the bran and germ removed and is often enriched with vitamins and iron. You can use either kind of cornmeal in this recipe. You'll need about ¹/₃ cup uncooked quinoa to make the ³/₄ cup cooked quinoa.

1¹/₂ cups stone-ground or degerminated cornmeal
³/₄ cup cooked quinoa (see page 98) or brown rice
¹/₂ cup whole wheat flour
1¹/₂ cups low-fat or nonfat buttermilk
2 tablespoons peanut or vegetable oil
1 teaspoon baking powder
¹/₂ teaspoon salt
¹/₂ teaspoon baking soda
3 egg whites

Heat oven to 450°. Grease square pan, 8 × 8 × 2 inches, or round pan, 9 × 1¹/₂ inches. Mix all ingredients; beat vigorously 30 seconds. Pour into pan. Bake 25 to 30 minutes or until golden brown. Serve warm. *9 servings.*

Nutrition Information Per Serving

1 serving		% of U.S. RDA	
Calories	170	Vitamin A	2%
Protein, g	6	Vitamin C	*
Carbohydrate, g	28	Thiamin	4%
Fat, g	4	Riboflavin	6%
Cholesterol, mg	0	Niacin	2%
Sodium, mg	290	Calcium	8%
Fiber, g	2	Iron	4%

Chocolate Chip–Date Coffee Cake

1¹/₂ cups packed brown sugar
¹/₃ cup margarine, softened
1¹/₂ teaspoons vanilla
5 egg whites or ³/₄ cup cholesterol-free egg product
1 cup all-purpose flour
1 cup whole wheat flour
1 cup oat or wheat bran
2 teaspoons baking powder
1 teaspoon baking soda
¹/₂ teaspoon salt
2 cups plain low-fat or nonfat yogurt
¹/₂ cup miniature semisweet chocolate chips
¹/₂ cup chopped dates
Glaze (right)

Heat oven to 350°. Spray 12-cup bundt cake pan or tube pan, 10 × 4 inches, with nonstick cooking spray. Beat brown sugar, margarine, vanilla and egg whites in large bowl on low speed until well blended. Beat on medium speed 2 minutes, scraping bowl occasionally. Beat in flours, oat bran, baking powder, baking soda and salt alternately with yogurt on low speed. Stir in chocolate chips and dates. Spread in pan.

Bake 55 to 60 minutes or until toothpick inserted near center comes out clean. Cool 20 minutes. Remove from pan; place on wire rack. Cool 30 minutes. Drizzle with Glaze. Serve warm or let stand until cool. *16 servings.*

GLAZE

¹/₂ cup powdered sugar
¹/₄ teaspoon vanilla
2 to 3 teaspoons skim milk

Mix all ingredients until smooth and drizzling consistency.

Nutrition Information Per Serving

1 serving		% of U.S. RDA	
Calories	275	Vitamin A	6%
Protein, g	6	Vitamin C	*
Carbohydrate, g	49	Thiamin	12%
Fat, g	6	Riboflavin	12%
Cholesterol, mg	0	Niacin	6%
Sodium, mg	260	Calcium	12%
Fiber, g	3	Iron	10%

Chocolate Chip–Date Coffee Cake

Pear-Streusel Coffee Cake

Streusel Topping (right)
³/₄ cup sugar
¹/₄ cup (¹/₂ stick) margarine, softened
1 teaspoon vanilla
3 egg whites or ¹/₂ cup cholesterol-free egg product
1³/₄ cups all-purpose flour
1 teaspoon baking powder
¹/₂ teaspoon baking soda
¹/₂ teaspoon ground cardamom
¹/₄ teaspoon salt
1 cup reduced-fat sour cream
2 cups chopped peeled pears (about 2 medium)
Glaze (right)

Heat oven to 350°. Spray rectangular pan, 13 × 9 × 2 inches, with nonstick cooking spray. Prepare Streusel Topping; reserve. Beat sugar, margarine, vanilla and egg whites in large bowl on medium speed 2 minutes, scraping bowl occasionally. Beat in flour, baking powder, baking soda, cardamom and salt alternately with sour cream on low speed. Fold in pears. Spread in pan. Sprinkle with Streusel Topping. Bake 45 to 55 minutes or until toothpick inserted in center comes out clean. Cool 15 minutes. Drizzle with Glaze. Serve warm or let stand until cool. *15 servings.*

STREUSEL TOPPING

2 tablespoons firm margarine
¹/₃ cup granulated sugar
¹/₃ cup packed brown sugar
2 tablespoons all-purpose flour
¹/₂ teaspoon ground cinnamon

Cut margarine into remaining ingredients with pastry blender until crumbly.

GLAZE

¹/₂ cup powdered sugar
¹/₄ teaspoon vanilla
2 to 3 teaspoons skim milk

Mix all ingredients until smooth and drizzling consistency.

Nutrition Information Per Serving

1 serving		% of U.S. RDA	
Calories	235	Vitamin A	8%
Protein, g	3	Vitamin C	*
Carbohydrate, g	42	Thiamin	10%
Fat, g	6	Riboflavin	10%
Cholesterol, mg	5	Niacin	4%
Sodium, mg	170	Calcium	4%
Fiber, g	1	Iron	6%

Applesause–Brown Rice Coffee Cake

Regular brown rice takes about 45 minutes to cook, while the quick-cooking variety takes only about 10 minutes. Either kind will make for a delicious coffee cake!

Topping (right)
1¹/₄ cups whole wheat flour
1 cup all-purpose flour
1 cup unsweetened applesauce
³/₄ cup packed brown sugar
2 tablespoons vegetable oil
1¹/₂ teaspoons baking powder
¹/₂ teaspoon ground cinnamon
¹/₂ teaspoon ground nutmeg
¹/₄ teaspoon baking soda
¹/₄ teaspoon salt
2 egg whites
¹/₂ cup chopped dried apples
¹/₂ cup cooked brown rice

Heat oven to 350°. Spray square pan, 9 × 9 × 2 inches, with nonstick cooking spray. Prepare Topping; reserve. Beat remaining ingredients except apples and rice in large bowl on low speed 30 seconds. Beat on medium speed 2 minutes, scraping bowl occasionally. Stir in apples and rice. Spread in pan. Sprinkle with Topping. Bake 35 to 40 minutes or until toothpick inserted in center comes out clean. Serve warm or let stand until cool. *9 servings*.

TOPPING

¹/₄ cup granulated sugar
¹/₄ cup packed brown sugar
¹/₂ teaspoon ground cinnamon

Mix all ingredients.

Nutrition Information Per Serving

1 serving		% of U.S. RDA	
Calories	300	Vitamin A	*
Protein, g	5	Vitamin C	*
Carbohydrate, g	61	Thiamin	12%
Fat, g	4	Riboflavin	8%
Cholesterol, mg	0	Niacin	10%
Sodium, mg	200	Calcium	6%
Fiber, g	3	Iron	12%

Raisin-Teff Coffee Cake

To make ½ cup cooked cornmeal, cook and stir ½ cup water and 3 tablespoons cornmeal in 1-quart saucepan over medium heat until mixture boils and thickens.

½ cup cooked teff or cornmeal
½ cup raisins
2 tablespoons honey
¼ cup (½ stick) firm margarine
1 cup all-purpose flour
1 cup whole wheat flour
2 tablespoons sugar
2½ teaspoons baking powder
½ teaspoon salt
About ¾ cup skim milk
Glaze (right)

Heat oven to 425°. Grease cookie sheet. Mix teff, raisins and honey; reserve. Cut margarine into flours, sugar, baking powder and salt with pastry blender in large bowl until mixture resembles fine crumbs. Stir in just enough milk so dough leaves side of bowl and forms a ball.

Turn dough onto lightly floured surface; gently roll in flour to coat. Knead lightly 10 times. Pat or roll dough into rectangle, 14 × 8 inches. Spread teff mixture over dough. Roll up tightly, beginning at 14-inch side. Pinch edge of dough into roll to seal. Shape into ring, seam side down, on cookie sheet; pinch ends together.

Make cuts with scissors ⅔ of the way through ring at 1-inch intervals. Turn each section on its side so filling shows. Bake 20 to 25 minutes or until golden brown. Remove from cookie sheet; place on wire rack. Cool 15 minutes. Drizzle with Glaze. Serve warm. *12 servings.*

GLAZE

⅓ cup powdered sugar
1½ teaspoons skim milk
⅛ teaspoon vanilla

Mix all ingredients until smooth.

Nutrition Information Per Serving

1 serving		% of U.S. RDA	
Calories	170	Vitamin A	2%
Protein, g	3	Vitamin C	*
Carbohydrate, g	31	Thiamin	8%
Fat, g	4	Riboflavin	4%
Cholesterol, mg	0	Niacin	6%
Sodium, mg	230	Calcium	6%
Fiber, g	2	Iron	6%

METRIC CONVERSION GUIDE

U.S. UNITS	CANADIAN METRIC	AUSTRALIAN METRIC
Volume		
1/4 teaspoon	1 mL	1 ml
1/2 teaspoon	2 mL	2 ml
1 teaspoon	5 mL	5 ml
1 tablespoon	15 mL	20 ml
1/4 cup	50 mL	60 ml
1/3 cup	75 mL	80 ml
1/2 cup	125 mL	125 ml
2/3 cup	150 mL	170 ml
3/4 cup	175 mL	190 ml
1 cup	250 mL	250 ml
1 quart	1 liter	1 liter
1 1/2 quarts	1.5 liter	1.5 liter
2 quarts	2 liters	2 liters
2 1/2 quarts	2.5 liters	2.5 liters
3 quarts	3 liters	3 liters
4 quarts	4 liters	4 liters
Weight		
1 ounce	30 grams	30 grams
2 ounces	55 grams	60 grams
3 ounces	85 grams	90 grams
4 ounces (1/4 pound)	115 grams	125 grams
8 ounces (1/2 pound)	225 grams	225 grams
16 ounces (1 pound)	455 grams	500 grams
1 pound	455 grams	1/2 kilogram

Measurements		Temperatures	
Inches	Centimeters	Fahrenheit	Celsius
1	2.5	32°	0°
2	5.0	212°	100°
3	7.5	250°	120°
4	10.0	275°	140°
5	12.5	300°	150°
6	15.0	325°	160°
7	17.5	350°	180°
8	20.5	375°	190°
9	23.0	400°	200°
10	25.5	425°	220°
11	28.0	450°	230°
12	30.5	475°	240°
13	33.0	500°	260°
14	35.5		
15	38.0		

NOTE
The recipes in this cookbook have not been developed or tested using metric measures. When converting recipes to metric, some variations in quality may be noted.

INDEX